SEA FURY

FROM THE COCKPIT, No 12

ALAN L LEAHY

DC PUBLICATIONS

Contents

INTRODUCTION 4

EVOLUTION 6

FROM THE COCKPIT *Captain Alan J. Leahy* CBE DSC 14

   Thumps and Scars *Chief Petty Officer A. J. Cork* 20
   Guiding the Exuberance *Commander Graeme Rowan-Thomson* 36
   Seafire to Sea Fury *Captain Fred Hefford* OBE DSC 38
   Mediterranean Bale-Out *Lieutenant-Commander Robert McCandless* DSC 40
   A Wonderful Experience *Lieutenant Bob Neill* 42
   The Colour of Adrenalin *Lieutenant-Commander Peter Sheppard* AFC 45
   Fate Takes a Hand *Sub-Lieutenant Peter Rainbird* CBE DL 51

Above: A Sea Fury F. B. Mk 11 of 736 Naval Air Squadron, late 1951 or early 1952. Based at RNAS Culdrose in Cornwall—hence the 'CW' tail code— and part of the Naval Air Fighter School, at peak strength this Squadron had more than four dozen Furies on its books, and it was through here that all would-be naval fighter pilots passed in order to learn how to fly the aircraft. Its sister-unit, 738 Squadron (also at Culdrose), taught Sea Fury pilots how to utilise their aircraft operationally.

INTO ACTION *Captain Alan J. Leahy* CBE DSC 54
    Korean Snowstorm *Lieutenant-Commander Robert McCandless* DSC 78
    Tale of a Trim Tab *Commander Robin Foster* OBE 79
    Friendly Fire *Lieutenant-Commander Tom Leece* 82
    International Co-operation *Lieutenant-Commander Robert McCandless* DSC 84
    Everybody's Favourite *Vice-Admiral Sir Edward Anson* KCB FRAeS 84

FRONT-LINE SEA FURY SQUADRONS 86
    Waterlogged *Commander J. H. ('Boot') Nethersole* 94

RNVR SEA FURY SQUADRONS 110

SECOND-LINE SEA FURY SQUADRONS 114

SEA FURY COLOURS 121
    Flown by the Author 124

INTRODUCTION

THERE have been many occasions since World War II when the Fleet Air Arm has been called upon to participate in armed conflict. The Suez Crisis in 1956 and the Falklands War of 1982 are perhaps the most striking examples, while in more recent years Royal Navy front-line squadrons have been deployed to Iraq and Afghanistan and have served in these theatres, too, with great distinction (if, generally speaking, scant acknowledgement). There have also been a number of other campaigns, mostly in the Far and Middle East, in which Royal Navy aviators have played an active and successful part, but one particular conflict has receded in the public's collective memory and understanding to the point that it is often referred to as 'the forgotten war'.

On 25 June 1950, North Korean forces began an invasion of their southern neighbour in the Korean peninsula, and two days later the United Nations passed a resolution requesting that member countries come to the assistance of South Korea in the form of military pressure in order to eject the interlopers. The verbal response was immediate and forceful, and within a matter of weeks this had materialised into action as the United States, Great Britain and a number of British Commonwealth nations mobilised their military assets and began to deploy to the Far East in support of the beleaguered South Koreans.

The geography of the Korean theatre was tailor-made for the projection of carrier-borne air power, since targets were for the most part within easy range of ship-based aircraft. Moreover, opposition in the form of enemy air activity and seaborne forces was so minimal as to be almost negligible, and thus, although routine early-warning and defensive measures were of course always maintained by the ships involved, the likelihood of the vessels coming to grief was not strong.

The turn of the decade caught the Royal Navy in a period of transition: the surviving wartime fleet carriers had either become worn out during that conflict and were being utilised as training aids or were otherwise in reserve, while their replacements, thanks to the colossal economic problems facing the nation in the immediate postwar years, were either delayed in their delivery or had been cancelled. The majority of the Fleet Air Arm's front-line operations were therefore being handled by the wartime light fleet carriers, and it fell to two of the principal naval

Above: The epitome of piston-engined naval fighter design: Hawker Sea Fury WE686 shows off its purposeful lines.
Left: Tucking up its undercarriage, the Royal Navy Historic Flight's original display Sea Fury, TF956, takes to the skies.

combat aircraft of the day, the Fairey Firefly and the Hawker Sea Fury, to undertake the responsibility of carrying the burden. Of the other fighter and strike aircraft that might have been committed, the de Havilland Sea Hornet was too large an aeroplane to be utilised in numbers on board the light fleet carriers, the Blackburn Firebrand was a specialist torpedo bomber and therefore by and large redundant, and the first-generation jets not only required special carrier modifications (for example, revised safety barriers) but until the end of the conflict were not, in the Fleet Air Arm at least, even a half-way proven concept.

Thus were the Sea Fury and the Firefly blooded in combat operations, for the most part in what would today be termed ground attack, close air support and reconnaissance duties, although on occasion in air-to-air sorties as well, especially after November 1950 when the Chinese entered the fray. In practice, although both these aircraft could be configured for all the rôles demanded of the carrier air groups, the Fireflies tended to undertake the reconnaissance and rocketing while the Sea Furies were employed in bombing and air defence; re-equipping the aircraft for different rôles was time-consuming and an inefficient use of manpower.

With the end of the Korean War in July 1953 the Sea Fury's involvement in hostilities also came to a conclusion, and it was swiftly replaced in the front line by the new jets coming into service. It continued to serve the Fleet Air Arm in various second-line capacities until the late 1950s and a handful lingered until 1962. Many, however, were refurbished by Hawker and sold on to a number of foreign air arms, and some of these continued to fly the aircraft into the 1970s.

The Sea Fury vies with the Sea Hornet not only as the fastest piston-engine aircraft ever to serve in the Royal Navy, but also as the naval aircraft that engendered the most delight in its pilots as a result of its speed, manœuvrability, responsiveness and magnificent handling qualities. None who flew it had a harsh word to say about it—and that accolade is rare indeed in the history of military aviation.

EVOLUTION

THROUGHOUT World War II, aircraft development proceeded at a hectic pace, driven by the requirements of war and the need for ever faster, more capable combat aircraft. More powerful engines, greater range, a more lethal armament and greater all-round versatility, however, brought with them inevitable increases in dimensions and greater all-up weights, and in order to investigate whether this trend could be arrested a number of proposals were put forward by various manufacturers in response to one of the Air Ministry's specifications, F.6/42 (the last two numerals denoting the year of issue).

At Kingston-upon-Thames, the Hawker design team looked at their latest fighter, the Tempest, which was about to enter quantity production for the Royal Air Force, and decided that by reducing the span of the wing centre section and making other adjustments it should be possible to bring down the empty weight of the airframe by a few hundred pounds without compromising the aircraft's general capabilities. The result was the Fury, a development of the so-called Tempest Light Fighter that had been the company's initial response to F.6/42 and was now being designed to the latter's successor, F.2/43.

Because of the huge pressure on engine availability during this time of intensive hostilities, various assorted Fury prototypes were produced. One aircraft, LA610, acted as an engine test-bed, being fitted with, progressively, a Rolls-Royce Griffon 85, a Griffon 81, a Bristol Centaurus XV radial, a

Left, upper: Prototype Fury LA610 in its original guise, fitted with a Rolls-Royce Griffon 85 engine and contra-rotating, three-blade propellers. The aircraft featured a massive annular air intake, and the vertical tail was of the original design configuration. It can perhaps be inferred from this photograph that, by the time it was taken, another engine arrangement, perhaps involving a Centaurus, had also been installed.

Left, lower: LA610 in its Sabre-engine configuration, though with its exhaust pipes removed and sealed off and its tail clamped, the aircraft apparently now surplus to requirements. This was the fastest of all the Furies, reputedly capable of 480mph in level flight.

Opposite, top: SR661 was the first of the three 'navalised' Furies (notice the arrester hook), although the RAF-style camouflage and serial-number presentation betray its service origins. The original squat tailfin was quickly revised so as to incorporate more rudder area as seen here, principally to reduce the aircraft's tendency to swing on take-off—although, as discussed later, this tendency was never wholly neutralised.

Right: The second Sea Fury prototype, SR666, which first flew on 12 October 1945. This was the first Sea Fury to be fitted for armament: notice the wing cannon, and the six mounting points (per wing) for the R/P rails.

Napier Sabre VA and, finally, a Sabre VII; NX798 and NX802 were fitted with, respectively, a Centaurus XII and a Centaurus XV initially, but were later re-fitted with Centaurus XVIIIs (the production engine); and VP207, added to the list somewhat later in the test programme, was powered by a Sabre VII. A fifth prototype aircraft, VP213, was uncompleted. Meanwhile, in response to a suggestion by Sydney Camm, Hawker's Chief Designer, a carrier-based version, also powered by a Centaurus, was given official blessing with the serving of Specification N.22/43; this variant was to be developed by Boulton Paul at Wolverhampton. Three prototypes were constructed, SR661, SR666 and VB857. All were 'navalised' Furies with arrester hooks, although SR661 lacked wing-folding, and all three were powered by Centaurus engines (it appears that there was never any question of either of the alternative Fury powerplants being adopted by the carrier-borne adaptation).

Contracts for 200 Furies and 200 'navalised' Furies were placed in April 1944, and by the end of the year the first completed aircraft had appeared and been flown, NX798 first taking to the air on 1 September 1944 and its sister aircraft LA610 on 27 November that year. However, with the end of the war in prospect, shortly after this the naval order was halved and by the time World War II had ended the order for the RAF's aircraft had been cancelled altogether.

The navalised Fury survived the axe, the first example, SR661, flying in February 1945; over the following twelve months, with the pace of development now considerably slackened, a second aircraft, SR666, made its first flight, joined by the only aircraft to be built by Bouton Paul, VB857, and, in the interim, the third Fury landplane, NX802. Owing to delays in the Sabre engine programme and to an

Left, upper: An early Sea Fury—its identity cannot, regrettably, be established—awaiting its engine and much of its systems. The main fuel tank is prominently visible in the upper forward fuselage.

Opposite, top: Only one Sea Fury was, in the event, manufactured by Boulton Paul, and this rather severely cropped photograph, showing VB857 sporting the original squat vertical tail, is one of the few to depict it. The aircraft was involved in intensive trials, especially those concerned with Rocket-Assisted Take-Off Gear (RATOG), and was also used by Hawker as a demonstration aircraft, helping, in particular, to win the Sea Fury export order for the Royal Netherlands Navy.

Right: Sea Fury TF895, the first production Mk X, in the summer of 1946 and awaiting its paintwork. By this time the extended fin had been incorporated into the design as standard, although the early four-blade propeller is still evident. A Hawker Tempest V is visible in the right background.

apparent loss of interest in the Griffon as a powerplant for the new fighter, all production Sea Furies were fitted with the Centaurus.

As is usual with a brand new aircraft, the trials and testing phase of the development cycle got under way, and at a fairly relaxed pace, while Hawker geared up for production: half the 100 machines on order would be designated Sea Fury F. Mk X and half F.B. Mk XI, the difference between the two being concerned chiefly, as the prefixes suggest, with an enhanced rôle for the latter variant; all these aircraft had serials in the 'TF' range.

With production aircraft coming off the line, service trials were begun in the spring of 1947, and it was clear even from the very early results that, in the Sea Fury, the Navy was about to receive quantities of new fighters that represented the very pinnacle of achievement in terms of piston-engined aircraft: the aircraft's top level speed proved to be in excess of 390 knots, its handling and manœuvrability in the air were superlative, and its foibles were relatively minor and readily addressed. There were some concerns about the swing on take-off, the aircraft's longitudinal stability and its low-speed and stalling characteristics, and the early flight tests revealed that engine vibration was a serious nuisance, but some straightforward 'fixes' by the manufacturer brought about the necessary improvements (although, as highlighted later in this book, the tendency to swing on take-off was never fully eliminated). In due course a two-seat training version, the T.20, was produced.

It is interesting to observe that, in the Sea Fury, the Fleet Air Arm yet again took into service an aircraft that had been designed primarily as a landplane; in terms of monoplanes at least, hitherto the only genuinely successful British-designed aircraft that had been built from the beginning as a carrier-based aeroplane had been the Fairey Firefly, though fortunately the 1950s brought forth a number of other types that came into this category. Apart from the Firefly, the Sea Fury's British-built near-contemporaries in front-line service were the Seafire and the Sea Hornet, both derived from landplanes, and the Firebrand, which, though conceived as a carrier aircraft, was, in the opinion of almost all naval pilots, limited in capability and, moreover, a deck-landing disaster.

The success of the Sea Fury, and its importance to the Fleet Air Arm, can be appreciated from the fact that further batches of new aircraft were ordered regularly through to 1951, the last aircraft being delivered to the Royal Naval Volunteer Reserve in 1954. In total, including trainers, over 700 aircraft were built for the Fleet Air Arm.

The Sea Fury was taken into service by a number of other air arms, most notably those of Australia, Canada and the Netherlands, all of which operated British-built light fleet carriers of similar configuration to those in the Royal Navy. It was also sold, in slightly modified form, to the air forces of Pakistan, Iraq and Egypt, while those of Burma and Cuba acquired some former RN Sea Furies in the late 1950s. West Germany bought some, mostly two-seaters, for target-towing, and a couple of the Iraqi aircraft later found their way to Morocco. After the military had no further use for it and surplus airframes became available, several Sea Furies were acquired for preservation, including preservation in flying condition. Modified by enthusiasts, a number of these latter became favoured as racing aircraft.

Left: Flaps at maximum droop, TF898, a production Mk X, comes to an abrupt halt during carrier compatibility trials on board HMS *Illustrious*, spring 1947. A number of modifications were introduced to the Sea Fury as a result of these trials, including the extended arrester hook seen here.
Main image: The Dutch Navy was a major customer for the Sea Fury, acquiring aircraft from both Hawker and from the licenced production run undertaken by Fokker. Designated Mk 50 and Mk 60, they differed only in minor respects (radio fit, etc) from the Fleet Air Arm's Mk X and Mk XI, respectively. In not untypical Sea Fury pose, these aircraft have had their engine shutters slid open to encourage cooling, thereby exposing some of the 'innards'.

Left, upper: It was considered that, to the uninitiated student pilot, the brute power of the Sea Fury could come as a jolt, having spent his training days flying relatively sedate piston-engine types, and therefore a two-seat, dual-control version of the Hawker fighter was produced. The prototype was flown in early 1948 and the design was quickly taken into service, although, in the event, it was used more for instrument flying training than type conversion *per se*. The T.20, as it was dubbed (the photograph depicts an example in primer finish), differed in appearance from the single-seater in having two tandem cockpits, separated by Perspex glazing, two instead of four 20mm cannon, a fixed tail-wheel and no arrester hook. The instructor could monitor the gun sight in the front cockpit by means of a rather ungainly periscope projecting into the airflow.

Left, lower. The West German authorities purchased a number of two-seat Sea Furies, and a sole single-seater, for use by the Deutsche Luftfahrt Beratungsdienst as a target facilities aircraft. They lacked the periscope of the standard T.20 and were painted red overall.

Below: Other, export orders for the Sea Fury included one from Burma, which took eighteen refurbished Sea Fury Mk Xs and three Mk 20s that had been retired from the Royal Navy. They were utilised for the most part as target-tugs. Two are seen here ready for delivery.

EVOLUTION

Left: Almost a hundred Sea Furies were supplied to Pakistan, including this two-seat trainer, designated Mk 61 by Hawker; single-seaters were classed as Mk 60s.

Below: The Sea Fury has enjoyed widespread preservation, and a number are still flown regularly. Perhaps the best known is VR930, which serves with the Royal Navy Historic Flight, based at RNAS Yeovilton in Somerset. Since this photograph was taken, the aircraft has been refinished as '110-Q' of 802 Squadron—to which unit it was first issued in 1948.

SPECIFICATIONS
HAWKER SEA FURY Mks X, XI and 20

Manufacturer:	Hawker Aircraft Ltd, Kingston-upon-Thames, Surrey. Final assembly at Langley, Buckinghamshire.
Chief Designer:	Sir Sydney Camm.
Powerplant:	One 18-cylinder Bristol Centaurus XVIII air-cooled radial engine developing 2,550hp (in medium supercharge gear) or 2,280bhp (at maximum power altitude in full supercharge gear).
Dimensions:	Length overall 34ft 7in (10.54m); wing span 38ft 4½in (11.70m) spread, 18ft 2in (5.54m) folded; height 14ft 9in (4.50m) with tail down and propeller at maximum height; wing area (gross) 280.0 sq ft (26.01m²).
Weights:	All-up (Mk XI, with 200gal/909l fuel) 12,300lb (5,580kg), (Mk 20, with 172gal/782l fuel) 12,100lb (5,490kg); take-off (Mk XI, max. fuel) 13,790lb (6,255kg), (Mk XI, max. load) 14,555lb (6,600kg).
Armament:	Four (Mk 20 two) 20mm Hispano cannon with 580rds/gun, plus (optionally) two 45gal (205l) underwing fuel tanks and two 1,000lb (454kg) or 500lb (227kg) bombs, or two 90gal (410l) fuel tanks, or up to twelve 60lb (27kg) or four 180lb (82kg) rocket projectiles, or napalm, smoke or practice bombs.
Performance:	Maximum speed (normal, at sea level) 325kts (374mph, 602kph), (normal, 20,000ft/6,100m) 390kts (449mph, 722kph); economical cruising speed (normal, sea level) 295kts (339mph, 546kph), (normal, 20,000ft) 270kts (311mph, 506kph); climb rate (normal, sea level) 4,300ft/min (1,310m/min); radius of action (normal, sea level) 310nm (357 miles, 575km), (long-range, sea level) 710nm (818 miles, 1,315km).
Number built:	729 (3 prototypes, 50 Mk Xs, 615 Mk XIs, 61 Mk 20s).

FROM THE COCKPIT

Captain Alan J. Leahy CBE DSC

TOWARDS the end of 1949 I was appointed to the School of Naval Air Warfare at RNAS St Merryn (HMS *Vulture*) on the Air Weapons Officers' course. This course lasted nine months and consisted of six months in the classroom dealing with targets, weapons and sighting for cannon, bombs and rockets, plus the effectiveness of the mixture. Flying and the practical application of classroom work came only after successful completion of the theoretical section. During lunchtime one day in December I was approached by one of the SNAW instructors, who asked me if I was still interested in a trip in a Sea Fury as they had one spare that afternoon. 'Yes, sir,' was the immediate answer, and I dashed off to find to find the Instructor Lieutenant and got permission to miss the afternoon class. Not much later the SNAW instructor left me strapped in the cockpit, saying. 'Have a good flight and don't forget to lock the tail wheel.' I knew a bit more about flying the Sea Fury than locking the tail wheel as I had obtained a copy of the Sea Fury Pilot's Notes and had spent some time studying it, and I had also spent some time in the cockpit, making sure that I knew what all the switches, dials and levers were for—which seemed like a good idea because there were, after all, a total of 107 of them.

Starting the engine was reasonably easy, although, unlike Merlins and Griffons, the big Centaurus radial required the pilot to prime the injectors and the cylinders. Warm-up was carried out at 1,200rpm until 120°C cylinder-head and 15°C oil temperatures had been reached before the constant-speed propeller, the supercharger and the magnetos were checked at zero boost. Taxying was also easy, though necessitating a gentle weave to make sure that there was nothing hidden beneath the nose. Before the aircraft was lined up on the runway the normal take-

Above: A glimpse at the main instrument panel of a Sea Fury Mk 11.
Below: Sea Fury Mk 11 WF619 on a proving flight prior to its delivery to the Fleet Air Arm in early 1951. Type designations for British military aircraft were changed from roman to arabic numerals in 1947 and generally introduced into service the following year. The colour schemes applied to the airframes, and the design and presentation of the national markings, were also revised at this time. Notice the VHF radio aerial atop the fin: most Sea Furies had this fitment on the fuselage, abaft the cockpit, but front-line aircraft began to dispense with the aerial altogether when UHF was introduced in the early 1950s.

off checks were completed—trim, mixture, pitch, fuel, flaps, gills, gyros, switches, instruments, oxygen, hood, harness and hydraulics; the final checks for take-off included full and free movement of the controls—and, of course, I had to lock the tail wheel.

Take-off was carried out at full power and the aircraft was allowed to fly off in a tail-down attitude. When I was comfortably airborne, the pitch lever was moved to auto before I reduced boost. The speed for maximum rate of climb was 165 knots with 2,700rpm and 9.5 inches boost. However as this was my first flight and the cloud base was 3,000 feet, I elected to climb at a more relaxed rate of 2,250rpm in auto and 165 knots. The cloud base did not encourage me to do much in the way of aerobatics, but I managed a couple of rolls and some steep turns, producing fantastic streams of vapour from the wing tips. Next I practised some slow flying with the wheels down (under 185 knots) and with the flaps fully down (under 140 knots). A normal approach would be carried out from 1,000 feet downwind with the rpm selected to 2,400, and after reducing the speed to 100 knots in my high-level

15

SEA FURY

circuits, I felt confident enough to come down and try the real thing. Turning downwind and reducing speed to about 130 knots and with the landing checks—brakes, brake pressures, fuel, flaps, wheels and tail wheel—carried out, I reduced my speed to 100 knots as the turn on to finals was executed. The landing may not have been perfect, but at least I did not bend my aircraft!

That was the beginning of my association with the Sea Fury. When I completed my final flight in a Fury I had accumulated a total of 786 hours in her and had carried out 272 deck landings—more than in any other aircraft type I have piloted before or since, in a total of just over 4,500 hours and 670 deck landings—and I had enjoyed most of the experience immensely. Some idea of the pleasure it gave me in the air can be summed up by relating a short episode. During my time as CO of 803 (Scimitar) Squadron, when disembarked at RNAS Lossiemouth (HMS *Fulmar*), ten years after I had first sat in a Sea Fury at St Merryn and five since I had last flown one, I was rung up one day by the Aircraft Holding Unit at the Station, where some Furies were being prepared for dispatch to Airwork, who looked after the Navy's fleet requirements. 'Sir, we are looking for a pilot to take a Fury up on a test flight. Can you help?' My instantaneous response was 'You do not need to make any more phone calls! I will be right over!' On taking off, the years since the last flight just melted away as we climbed away to play . . . er, sorry, carry out the test flight. During the air test I spent a very happy time delighting in the Sea Fury's superb handling and aerobatic qualities. After landing, and during the debriefing with the Chief Aircraft Artificer, I suggested that the aircraft might require a second test flight as during high-g turns the port undercarriage red light had flickered. This could mean that the undercarriage was unlocked, but more usually it meant that the undercarriage fairing was being pulled out of its fully closed position by the combination of the high g and slipstream. We agreed that we could not dispatch the aircraft in that condition. After some gentle fettling and a successful test flight, the Chief and I reluctantly came to the conclusion that we would be pushing our luck if we said that it would require yet another test flight before it could go south to Airwork!

* * *

Following completion of the classroom section of the AWO course, we students were sent to the 52nd Training Air Group at RNAS Culdrose (HMS *Seahawk*). Most of the course was completed on Seafire 17s, but as time went by the Sea Fury featured more often in our logbooks. After graduation we moved on to our new appointments. Mine was to 736 Squadron, where student pilots were introduced to the Sea Fury, and then 738 Squadron as an Air Weapons Instructor. 738 Squadron's task was weapons training for new pilots and others who had been away from the front line before they moved on

Left: The final Sea Fury off the production line, flying here with 1833 Squadron (part of the Midland Air Division, Royal Naval Volunteer Reserve) as '158/BR'. Notice the wing-tip vortices, alluded to by the author.
Below: Another view of WF619. Glossy finishes were now *de rigueur*: they were more resistant to wear, and, more importantly, could offer the aircraft a few more knots of speed.

to their front-line squadrons. Both 736 and 738 had a mixture of Seafire 17s and Sea Furies, and as most of the students were bound for Sea Fury squadrons the instructors ended up in Seafires a lot of the time. It was very evident that there was a step change in the performance between the two aircraft.

In 736 Squadron, the student pilots who had recently received their wings were moving on from the Seafire 17 to the Sea Fury. This involved, first, a comprehensive series of lectures to ensure that they knew how the aircraft systems worked. Next they were introduced to the aircraft itself—how to carry out an external inspection before climbing into the cockpit, where they would learn where all the switches were located before undergoing a 'Blindfold Cockpit Check'. At this time we had a few Sea Fury two-seaters at Culdrose, but they were not used to give the students dual before flying the Sea Fury itself despite the fact that these aircraft were designed to be used as a 'step' between the basic trainer aircraft and the much more powerful front-line fighter. The Royal Navy's two-seat Fury sported a mirror mounted above and between the two cockpits, and this was to be used for weapons training: the instructor, sitting in the back seat, would stare at the device in order to monitor the student's gun sight in an attack. I do not remember any of my friends or myself taking part in this sport of assessment as I cannot imagine anything more foolhardy than diving headlong at a target using a mirror as a reference. The T.20 trainer was marvellous for instrument flying training and useful for demonstrating, at height, the dangers of getting too slow—less than 90 knots—on the approach to land and then suddenly opening up the throttle to full power (as a result of which, with the wings just about to stall, the five-

Main image: A Sea Fury Mk 11 assigned to 738 Squadron, equipped with R/P rails and carrying the RNAS Culdrose code letters on its tailfin, 1950. Earlier in its career, this aircraft has been based at RNAS St Merryn with 736 Squadron.
Inset: T.20 trainer VX818, the two-seat Sea Fury prototype. The standard finish for these trainers was aluminium overall, with yellow bands chordwise across the wings and around the after fuselage.

Above: Rear view of a Sea Fury trainer, offering a clear indication of the geometry of the Centaurus's exhaust system. Also visible, sprung out on the starboard side, is the retractable footstep aiding access to the front cockpit.

bladed-propeller, with 2,500 horsepower available from the Centaurus engine behind it, would 'grab' the air and flip the aircraft on to its back). With all the lectures and briefings satisfactorily completed, the student would be authorised for his first solo.

Once the student had signed Form 700—the aircraft's servicing record—denoting his acceptance of his mount, and had noted any entries made in red ink (which drew his attention to any very minor deficiencies that might be present on the aircraft but would not compromise its safety), he would, prior to boarding, carry out the routine walk-round check, principally to ensure that the aircraft's control surfaces were moving freely and that no red flags or tags were present. The crew entry step beneath the port wing root needed to be pulled down for the first stage en route to the spring-loaded step in the wing and from there to a step on the side of the cockpit which was open when the wheels were down. Once in the cockpit and sitting on the dinghy and parachute, he could then fasten himself to the dinghy (three clips), then to the parachute and finally to the aircraft's seat harness. The Pilot's Mate

Thumps and Scars *Chief Petty Officer A. J. Cork*

One morning when I was a young lad, and considered reliable enough to sign Form A700 (or was I?), an exercise was to take place and a rush was on to do the Daily Inspections and have the aircraft ready, out of the hangar and on to the apron. All those familiar with the cockpit layout of the Sea Fury know that the starter button is on the starboard shelf, next to the cylinder priming and injector buttons—which have to be tested in the Inspection. Unfortunately I pressed the wrong button, which immediately took the rudder off the aircraft in front of mine. As they say, 'There ain't no mercy with a Coffman starter!' The starter was a fine piece of gear, but it would occasionally malfunction, requiring the Pilot's Mate to 'persuade' the recalcitrant mechanism using a lump of phosphor bronze which was thumped against the body of the starter. This normally worked well.

I also recall one particularly awkward job—removing of the banjo union and associated tube to the oil pressure gauge. The process involved going into the cockpit head-first and getting one's head to the back of the port rudder pedal, and then releasing six 6BA screws. This was very trying—and indeed unendurable when somebody came along and decided to test the rudder for 'fill and free movement' to the left and right!

Another awkward job, usually carried out in a hurry, was changing the internal batteries. This process was not without a vicious hazard—the ZBX radio (the receiver for the homing YG signals broadcast by a carrier or shore station) had its aerial just aft of the bottom panel and appeared to have been designed to pierce the ribcage and lungs of anyone unfortunate enough to forget about it. I have a scar to prove it!

Above: 'Chocks away!' captured for posterity as the phrase was spoken. This is Mk XI VR944, a part of the smallest, and shortest-lived, front-line Sea Fury squadron, 806 (see page 100). The checks have been completed and the aircraft is ready to fly. Notice that the engine cooling shutters, immediately abaft the bare-metal, fixed protective plates adjacent to the exhaust outlets, have been slid open. This was standard procedure just before take-off, but the shutters were frequently kept open by pilots during flight (although it was recommended that they be closed for landing).
Below: A victim of engine failure: VX687 of 738 Squadron having come to grief after taking off from Culdrose in February 1951.

would help him to do all this, and would also assist him to connect the R/T and oxygen. From that point the student was on his own.

To my knowledge, all the students completed their familiarisation flights without any accidents—which, I suppose, says as much for the Sea Fury as it says for its pilots. The aircraft did not, however, have a fault-free history up to this time, as among the first fifty Sea Furies delivered to the Navy there had been at least fifteen engine failures and four pilots had been killed. There was a degree of warning if the Centaurus was in difficulty—the oil pressure would drop off the scale and the oil temperature would go up alarmingly, accompanied by some serious rough running—but whether the warnings came together or separately did not matter as there was nothing the pilot could do to avert an engine failure. This history came to mind one day just after I had taken off from

RNAS Culdrose with two 500-pound bombs. I was just crossing the airfield boundary, climbing away with the wheels locking up, when the engine went very quiet. It did not occur to me to check whether the oil temperature and pressure were all right because just ahead was the sea, which I hoped I could reach in time so as to jettison the bombs before ditching. Just after crossing the beach, I duly dispatched the bombs and was preparing to ditch when, suddenly, the engine roared back into life. Turning and climbing back to a high downwind, and thanking my good fortune, I landed and taxied back to dispersal with the engine ticking over as normal. Luckily, my story was backed up by one of the air traffic controllers, who had heard the engine stop and was about to sound the crash alarm just before he saw the aircraft climb away after the bombs were released.

Carrier operations, of course, called for some refinements to the basic take-off and landing procedures, and these were practised on the training carrier whenever it was available. Before they were attempted, however, a programme of Aerodrome Dummy Deck Landings (ADDLs), together with careful briefings, was designed to ensure that the student acted in accordance with signals given to him by the Deck Landing Control Officer (DLCO, or 'batsman') and ended up safely on board. Part of the instruction reminded the later Sea Fury pilots of the demonstration in the trainer before their first solo with the instructor in the front seat. The situation could occur close to the deck when the batsman realised that the approaching aircraft was getting dangerously low and slow and signalled to the pilot that he should add power and climb. It was vital to make sure that lots of left rudder was fed in to counter the sudden rise in power. This was not easy to remember on a novice pilot's first approach to the deck when he had a great number of new things to think about.

However, provided these 'rules' were meticulously observed, landing a Sea Fury on board a carrier was

Left, upper: With good reason, carrier landings by naval aircraft are sometimes described as 'controlled crashes', and the techniques called for—not least familiarity with the signals of the DLCO—needed to be mastered on land before they could be applied at sea. Hence the famous and inevitable ADDLs (Aerodrome Dummy Deck Landings) that all had to practise before deploying on board ship. Here the batsman indicates to an approaching Sea Fury pilot that he is 'Steady', i.e., in the correct position.

Left, lower: On the point of taking the wire, Sea Fury WM494 (807 Squadron) executes a textbook landing on board the light fleet carrier HMS Ocean, 1953.

Opposite, top: WJ277 (801 Squadron, HMS Glory) is hauled to a halt by the arrester wire as a deck hand dashes forward to assist in the aircraft's recovery, off Korea in 1952.

Opposite, bottom: F. B. Mk 11 WE785 (810 NAS) in three-point attitude but apparently having missed the wires on board the new carrier HMS Centaur, summer 1954. It was standard practice for a pilot to slide his canopy back when coming into land: this facilitated his rescue in the event of an accident.

Overleaf: The famous wartime fleet carrier HMS Illustrious, widely employed postwar in hosting trials aircraft, about to receive a Sea Fury, circa 1947. The safety barriers are rigged amidships. The batsman can just be discerned, signalling 'Go port' to help the pilot to align his aircraft more precisely

a relatively trouble-free affair—certainly when compared with some of the interesting touch-downs that were the lot of the Seafire. The latter was a temperamental deck-landing aircraft, with a tendency to jump hither and thither once its wheels had met the flight deck. In comparison, the Fury was generally solid and reliable. It still did have one little trick up its sleeve, however. The pilot would make his approach just above the stall, with power on and in perfect three-point attitude, ready to 'Cut' when the batsman gave the signal. When the 'Cut' was taken, the nose of the aircraft would, if left to its own devices, nod down, the main wheels would strike the deck first and the tail hook would sail over the arrester wires, the end result being an aircraft bouncing straight into the barrier. The solution was for the pilot to pull back hard on the stick so as to get the aircraft down in a three-point attitude and let the

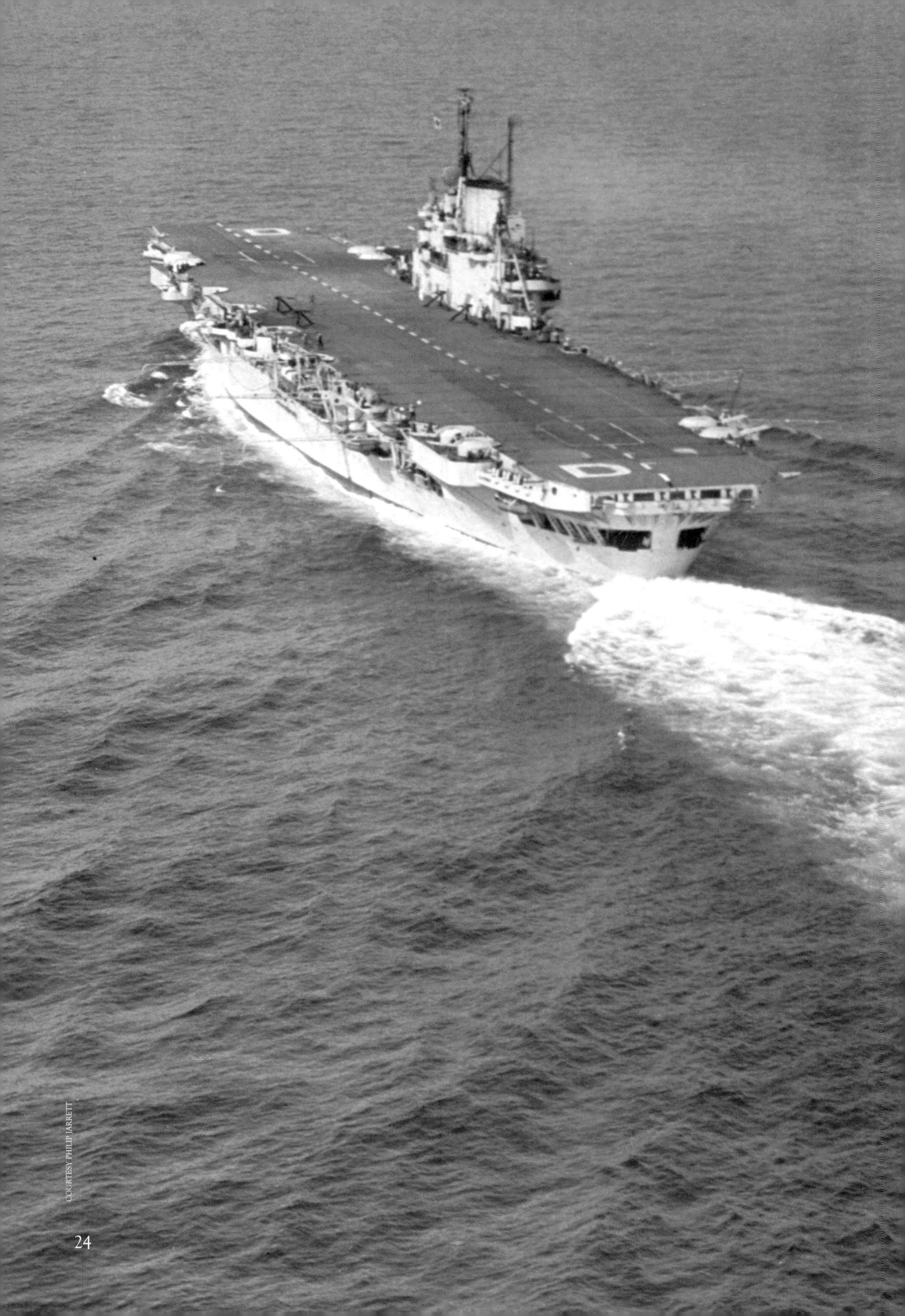

COURTESY PHILIP JARRETT

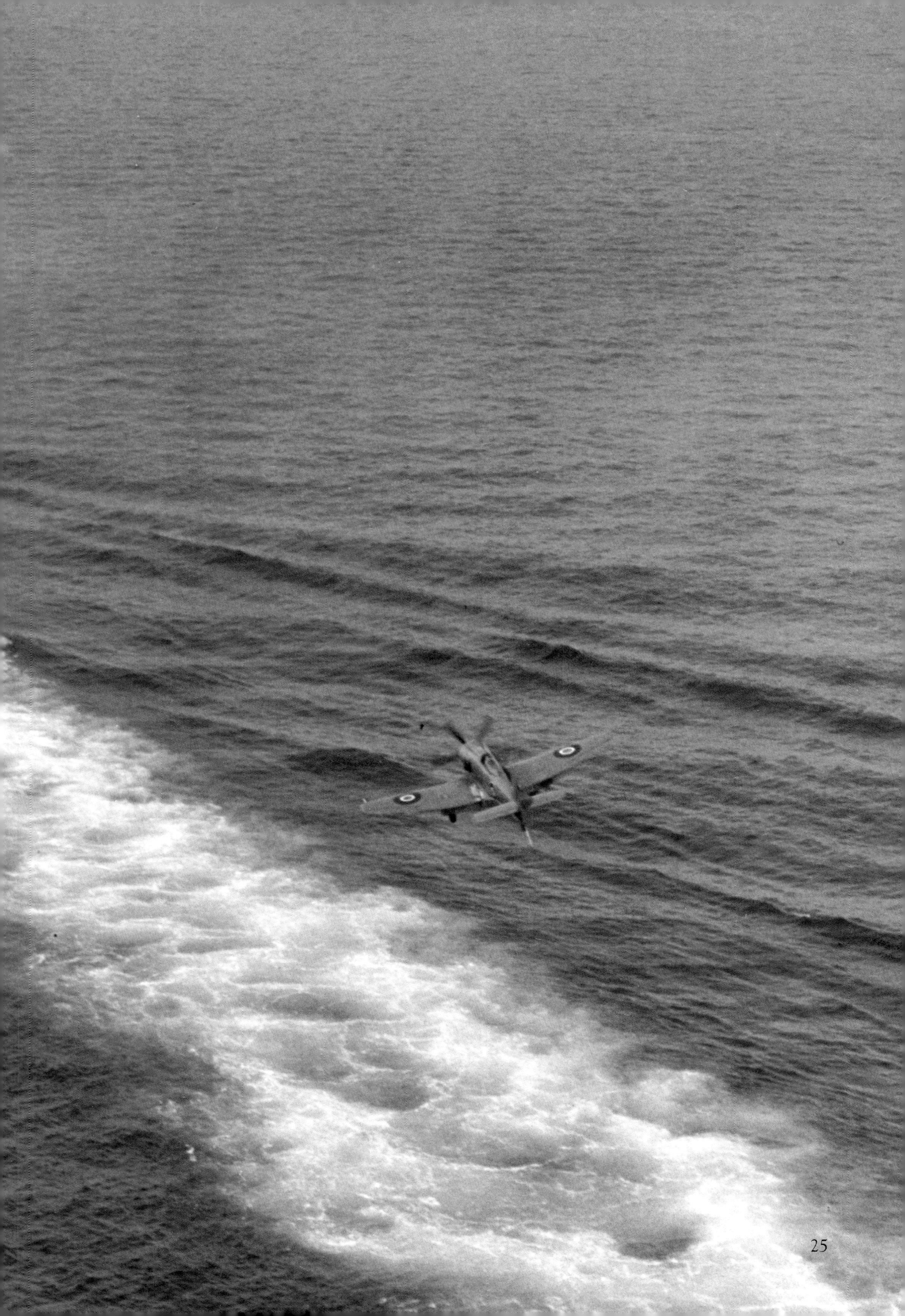

hook catch the wire. Pulling back hard with a barrier and a deck park of aircraft and people a couple of hundred feet in front of you is not the easiest thing to get your head around.

The deck-landing circuit was different from, and lower than, that of the airfield. The downwind leg was conducted at 400 feet with 2,400rpm set, full flap, 'four greens' (wheels down, hook down) and tail wheel unlocked. Carrier landings in a Fury had to be accomplished with the tail wheel unlocked because if the landing was slightly imperfect (i.e., not straight down the middle of the deck), the arrester wire would be caught off-centre and the arrester gear would then try to even the strain on the two sheaves on the ends of the arrester wire itself. The resulting strain on a locked tail wheel could be enough to cause serious damage to the tail wheel assembly. This vital difference was, one might have thought, easy to remember, but pilots nevertheless occasionally forgot—especially if, when operating at sea, they had an emergency that obliged them to divert to a nearby land base, where, instead of leaving the tail wheel unlocked, it was prudent to lock it.

With the airspeed at 130 knots, the turn crosswind would begin when the pilot was level with the back of the carrier's island. The batsman, who had two ratings with him by his platform, would be informed by the first, who was watching the aircraft through his binoculars: 'Wheels down, hook down, flaps down, sir.' Boost would be approximately –1psi turning in, decreasing to about –3 towards the latter stages of the approach as the turn was slackened with the speed at 90–92 knots. The second man would be looking forward, watching the aircraft that had just landed and waiting for aircraft's hook to be

Above: A *contretemps* with the safety barrier for VW714 (738 Squadron) during deck landing training on board HMS *Illustrious*, July 1952.
Right, top: A last (tenth)-wire arrest but a safety barrier encounter nevertheless for VW661 of 804 Squadron on board HMS *Glory* in May 1951, brought about as a result of too speedy an approach to land-on.
Right, centre: An engine run for WE725 of 811 Squadron on board HMS *Warrior*, 1954. Notice the camera installation in the fuselage adjacent to the wing trailing edge.
Right, bottom: Fully armed, 801 Squadron's Sea Furies prepare to take off from HMS *Glory*, winter 1952/53. The leading aircraft has had its starboard fuel tank locally modified to accept a reconnaissance camera; 500-pound bombs are outboard.

Left: 'Bats' in action: Lieutenant Tony Lacayo, Deck Landing Control Officer, on board HMS *Glory*. His companion here is Lieutenant 'Pug' Mather, who, during the Korean War, had the misfortune of being twice shot down and spent some time as a prisoner-of-war.

FROM THE COCKPIT

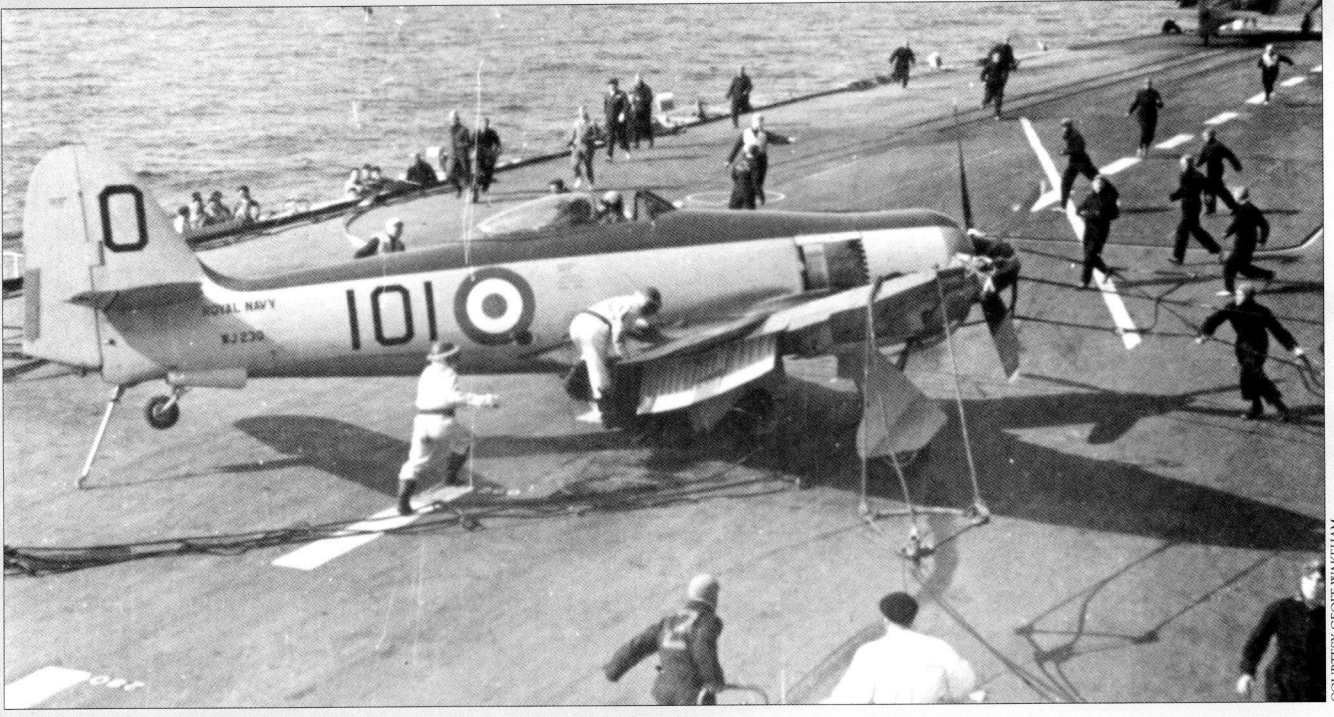

disengaged from the wires, the aircraft to clear the barrier and the barrier to be raised; he would call as the batsman controlled the next aircraft, 'Wires up, barriers up, green light affirmative, sir.' These men were vital members of the team, especially when a worked-up air group was landing on with approximately 25 seconds between each of the landings. During deck-landing training, of course, such intervals were not wanted.

After a safe landing, the student's next task was to fly off the deck safely. There were three kinds of take-offs that needed to be learned: a free take-off would be made when there was a clear deck, the second method was via the catapult and the third method was accomplished with the assistance of Rocket Assisted Take-Off Gear (RATOG). At Culdrose there was no means of demonstrating catapult take-offs, and both briefing and execution, therefore, took place on board ship. Once the aircraft had been started up and all take-off checks had been completed as for a land-based departure—but with the flaps at maximum lift and the tail wheel unlocked—the Fury would be taxied on to the catapult, where the catapult strop and the hold-back would be attached to the airframe. The catapult shuttle would then be tensioned ready to launch. Using his green

FROM THE COCKPIT

Left, upper: Despite the intensive training, and despite the plethora of safety precautions, deck landing accidents were frequent occurrences even in front-line squadrons. This is a 'prang' involving 898 Squadron's WE693, which missed the wires and was halted by the barrier during a landing on board *Ocean* on 11 December 1952. The recovery crane has also come to grief.

Left, lower: Another landing mishap on board HMS *Ocean*, this time involving WJ230 of 802 Squadron, 19 February 1952.

This page: A sequence of photographs depicting the fiery end of WE716—from which the pilot, fortunately, escaped. The aircraft took the wire, but the after fuselage suddenly broke away and the rest of the airframe somersaulted and crashed, losing its engine in the process. The remains were consigned to the deep. 801 Squadron, HMS *Indomitable*, October 1951.

flag, the Flight Deck Officer (FDO) would signal for the pilot to raise full power. The pilot would signal when he was ready to launch and tuck his right elbow into his stomach, holding on to the control column, and with his left hand holding the throttle fully open would wait while the FDO slowly lowered his green flag to signal that the catapult should be fired. The pilot's particular body posture was designed to prevent the stick from being pulled back and pitching the aircraft up after the sudden and startling acceleration when the catapult had fired.

Above: A war-worn Sea Fury ('130-T', serial number unidentified) awaits launch from the carrier *Theseus*. The man with the green flag is standing by the port catwalk and will have to duck sharply once he has signalled. The black and white striping was characteristic of—though by no means universally applied to—Sea Furies taking part in the Korean operations.
Below: Sea Fury Mk X TF973 (807 Squadron) about to receive the signal to launch from *Theseus*'s catapult, *circa* 1948. The catapult strop is clearly visible, and the hold-back device can be seen deployed beneath the aircraft's arrester hook.
Right, upper: 804 Squadron's VX624 departs from HMS *Glory*, early 1951, leaving the catapult strop on deck.
Right, lower: A rocket-laden VR943 leaves HMS *Glory*, spring 1951. The Sea Fury's flaps needed to be deployed for catapult launches, though not for departures from fixed runways. Here the port main undercarriage unit has already started to retract.

Once airborne the aircraft was easy to clean up by putting the wheels and flaps up and switching the rpm to auto.

With the introduction to carrier operations completed, the course would return to continue with its training ashore. Not all courses went smoothly, however. On one occasion the pilot got low and slow as he approached the round-down, and when the batsman signalled for more power the aircraft rolled over to starboard and crashed, inverted, in the sea. The pilot was not recovered.

After completing their time in 736 Squadron, the students moved over to 738 Squadron, where they were to introduced to the aircraft's weapons. The Sea Fury was equipped with four 20mm cannon, and when the Mk 11 came along the aircraft was also capable of carrying two 500-pound or two 1,000-pound bombs. It could, alternatively, carry twelve three-inch rockets with 60-pound high-explosive warheads. However, a rôle change from bombs to rockets or *vice-versa* was expensive in terms of maintenance hours.

There were two vital components in the method of teaching pilots how use the aircraft's weapons: the first was the camera gun sight and the second the Wren Range Assessor. Before anyone was allowed to fire off any weapons it was essential to ensure that there was a reasonable chance that the unleashed projectiles would end up where they were meant to go. When strafing a ground target with his cannon,

Above: Another view of VX639 (see pages 18-19) up from Culdrose while assigned to 738 Squadron, here carrying 60-pound rockets with concrete heads and, no doubt, bound for Treligga to deliver them. Four of the six available R/P stations are being utilised here.
Below: Sea Fury pilots in the making: the personnel of 736 Squadron at Culdrose in 1951. The CO at the time was Lieutenant-Commander P. M. Austin, and the author is seated ninth from the left.
Right: Occasionally a student pilot would be involved in a mishap, as befell Sub-Lieutenant G. J. K. Greenlaw when his Sea Fury's undercarriage gave way on landing at Culdrose on 24 February 1953. The pilot was unhurt and the aircraft was later repaired and returned to service.

the pilot was taught to fire from a 20-degree dive using the fixed ring-and-cross in the gun sight; less than 20 degrees meant that he was taking the risk that debris from the target or ricochets would meet him as he pulled up. When firing at an airborne target, the gyro part of the sight would be used. The picture of the sight was a centre spot with nine diamonds in a circle round it. By setting the wing span of the target on the sight and then twisting the grip on the throttle to encircle the target, the pilot gave the sight the range of the target and then the sight would work out the deflection required to hit it. It was here that the Wrens came into the picture: they assessed the film and had to tell the pilot that he was not the 'ace' that he thought he might have been. The next step was to fire, using the fixed ring, at a drogue towed by a Martinet target tug. The 20mm shells would have different coloured inks painted on their tips so that each pilot's score could be counted. This was not an easy exercise either.

Before firing any rockets or dropping any bombs it was again necessary to see that the pilot had mastered the skills required. At a nearby disused airfield a series of three large-diameter rings was painted on the ground and the pilot would dive on the rings with his camera gun running. Once more the Wrens came into their own, because they were able to calculate the angle of dive, the height of release and the point of aim. For rocketing we taught an angle of dive of 30 degrees and a release height of 1,500 feet, and for dive-bombing an angle of dive of 65 degrees and a release height of 3,500 feet. For low-level bombing the rule was 'low, but not too low'! Live firing took place, for air-to-air, off the Cornish coast north of Padstow, while for rocketing and bombing we used the Treligga Range on the coast and the Wrens plotted the fall of shot and reported it to the pilot after each dive. The rockets used for practice were the three-inch type with 60-pound concrete heads. When bombing, 11.5-pound bomb racks, each carrying four bombs, were fitted to the normal bomb racks.

After successfully completing this part of the course, the pilot was considered qualified to be appointed to a first-line squadron.

FROM THE COCKPIT

Opposite page: A manufacturer's publicity photograph showing the range of underwing stores that the Sea Fury could lift. The large 90-gallon drop tanks are tucked in hard against the undercarriage legs, with the smaller and more commonly used 45-gallon tanks alongside.
Above: A much-published photograph showing a quartet of Sea Furies of 805 Squadron ('Q' for HMS *Vengeance*) at the time of the changeover in Fleet Air Arm colour schemes and markings. The new scheme comprised Sky Type 'S' (a pale green) under surfaces and fuselage sides, with Extra Dark Sea Grey upper surfaces; the original Sea Fury scheme, displayed by three of the aircraft here, is generally described as having employed the same colours, but with the Extra Dark Sea Grey taken down the fuselage sides and covering the tailfin. However, there is evidence to suggest that, on some aircraft at least, the uppersurfaces may in fact have been camouflaged with a disruptive pattern of Extra Dark Sea Grey and Dark Slate Grey, in a continuation of the late wartime pattern. The difficulty is that it is virtually impossible to distinguish between these two colours in the majority of monochrome photographs, especially where the paintwork is glossy in character.
Below: The Sea Furies of 802 Squadron in 1953, photographed at RNAS Hal Far, Malta; the aircraft are assigned to the carrier HMS *Theseus* ('T'). Type 'D' roundels replaced the Type 'C' (on the wings) and Type 'C1' (on the fuselage) cockades with the introduction of the new paint scheme, and fin flashes were was dispensed with.

35

SEA FURY

Guiding the Exuberance *Commander Graeme Rowan-Thomson*

Our next move in the training system was down to Culdrose, where we were to learn advanced battle tactics and live weapon-firing, and—the ultimate—finish off with our introduction to real, live deck-landings on a real, live carrier operating off Land's End. This part, like that at Lossie, would occupy about three months.

We were now, also, approaching a danger point in our flying careers. We had flown a front-line aircraft, the Seafire, we had around 170 total solo hours and we had our Wings. We were part of the élite—and we knew all the answers! This was a heady mixture which could very easily lead to disaster if unchecked on the spot. It did not affect all the young, embryonic pilots, only those whose basic philosophy was 'Kick the tyres, light the fires, and the last one up to thirty grand's a cissy!' I was of that breed!

It was not a criminal offence. The thrill and exuberance of flying, the sheer joy of throwing an aircraft around in space and swooping amongst the fluffy clouds—this was what you had joined for, and here it was, but luckily there were wise heads around the place who jumped, sometimes quite hard, on stupidity and a know-it-all approach and guided the exuberance in the right direction. Take risks, yes, but know what you're doing.

At Culdrose we converted on to the current fleet front-line fighter-bomber, the Sea Fury. She was a beautiful aircraft with a radial engine and a five-bladed propeller to absorb the 2,500hp the engine produced. The Seafire had a very 'busy' engine even when you were just cruising, but the first time I throttled back to 'cruise' in the Sea Fury I thought the engine had stopped; it was a very lazy rotation. The Fury had been with the fleet for some four years and was to carry the Royal Navy through the Korean War with flying colours. In retrospect, it has been assessed as one of the outstanding piston-engined fighters of all time, if not the best.

However, with advanced aircraft come advanced risks, and my first shock was when once, just after take-off, I was climbing away from the runway and my engine really did stop! I was so horrified that all I could do was yell 'My engine's failed!' over the radio, whereupon I was told by the Control Tower that I could land on any runway I liked. I was about to tell them that the sea or a ploughed field were the only options when the engine picked up again with a roar. In reality, it had probably only stopped for about two seconds—but they were awfully long seconds!

We did a lot of weapons training, firing cannon and rockets and dropping 25-pound practice bombs, and it was on one of these sorties that I learned another lesson. The usual method of attacking with rockets was to go into a 30-degree dive and at a certain height (800 feet) and a certain speed (300 knots) fire the rockets and pull firmly out of the dive, firstly to avoid hitting the ground and secondly to avoid flying through any debris thrown up by the exploding ordnance. Towards the end of the course the training Squadron Commander, one Pete Austin, decided to lead the whole course on a simulated attack on a nearby range. We took off in stream, joined up,

COURTESY PHILIP JARRETT

Above: Sea Furies F.B.11s and T.20s of 738 Squadron run up their engines at Culdrose in 1953.
Below: Another view of the 736/738 Squadron flight line at Culdrose, this time circa 1950–51. The nearest aircraft later served with the Royal Australian Navy in 805 Squadron.

flew around the countryside for a bit and then, one section after another, flew on to the range and into the dive. Sights on the target, right height, right speed, press the button and *whoosh!* Four rockets plunged to earth. I was determined to hit the target, and as I pulled out of the dive—a bit low, perhaps—I felt sure that I had. And that thump I'd felt was probably a pocket of air. We all joined up again and then, some sixteen aircraft in four groups of four, flew back to Culdrose to join the circuit and land, led by Pete Austin. I was in the third group, so we had to circle the airfield whilst the first two did their circuit drill and started landing on the runway.

It was at that moment that I happened to cast a quick look at my instruments—not an easy job when you are flying in tight formation.

To my horror I saw that the cylinder-head temperature had climbed into the red sector and was going on up, whilst my oil pressure gauge was showing zero. I had lost all my coolant oil and the engine was going to stop abruptly in the near future—in seconds rather than minutes! I then found that my radio transmitter had packed up so I couldn't tell anyone what had happened or what I was doing—which was to land as soon as possible. I broke away from my section, cut into the pattern of aircraft in the circuit and pushed to the head of the queue. The lead aircraft, Austin, had just landed but my speed was such that I had to leapfrog over him and land ahead of him!

Back in dispersal it could be seen there was a jagged hole in my oil-cooler radiator and rivulets of oil going back along the fuselage. I was hoping the ground would open up and swallow me but, surprisingly, everyone seemed rather relaxed about it all. I'd heard one of the section leaders say 'I think he's got trouble' as I peeled away, but I had landed without incident, no one had got hurt, and I had a comparatively light mauling from Peter Austin on the lines of 'Look what happens when you fly into your own rocket debris' (only phrased rather more graphically!).

37

Seafire to Sea Fury Captain Fred Hefford OBE DSC

The Seafire, which was a delight to fly, had performed well in Fleet Air Arm service, but the Admiralty's Department of Naval Air Warfare had seen the need for an aircraft with an even better performance, increased range and a greater weapon load. They had chosen the Hawker Sea Fury, fitted with the very powerful Bristol Centaurus 18 sleeve-valve radial engine, driving a Dowty five-bladed propeller. The Sea Fury Mks 10 and 11 were about to begin flying from HMS *Theseus*, as part of the United Nations Force in Korea, soon after Mick Fieldhouse, Mike Darlington and I arrived back in Britain from HMS *Triumph*, to join the K3 Sea Fury Conversion and Fighter Course at the 52nd Training Air Group, Naval Air Fighter School, RNAS Culdrose.

Our first close-up encounter with the aircraft showed us that the Sea Fury, with its big radial engine, dwarfed the Seafire, and that the undercarriage, unlike that on the Seafire, looked sturdy and widely spaced. We were no longer able simply to step up on to the wing-walk in order to gain access to the cockpit, but found instead, just behind the wing root, a stirrup step that automatically lowered whenever the undercarriage was selected down. We discovered that the cockpit was voluminous compared with that of any aircraft we had previously flown.

The instruments and cockpit layout were familiar, but there were many ergonomic improvements, such as simplifying the actions required to raise and lower the undercarriage, an easily operated wing-fold/wing-spread control and a tailwheel lock. The last was necessary to help with directional control on take-off and landing.

Under the guidance of the Aircraft Directors, taxying the aircraft was easy, using the conventional pneumatic brakes, controlled with a lever attached to the stick and differential braking by rudder-pedal movement, but, like all powerful single-engine, tailwheel aircraft of the day, it was necessary to weave when taxying, in order to ensure that no obstructions lay ahead.

The first take-off was a revelation, with the extra vital action of locking the tailwheel and gently opening the throttle until the rudder was able to provide adequate directional control. With the stick well back, and with the pilot steadily opening up to full power, the aircraft accelerated with a throaty roar from the Centaurus, a gentle easing forward of the stick brought the tail up and hey presto!—the Fury, a masterpiece of engineering and aerodynamics, was soon airborne.

Once the aircraft was off the ground, the splendid view from the cockpit, allowed by the large bubble canopy and the taper of the fuselage from cockpit to engine, was a pleasant surprise. The performance and handling characteristics of the aircraft were superb and gave us confidence in our ability to fulfil our rôle.

We had been briefed that torque-stall could occur if power had to be applied because the aircraft had been allowed to get too slow and too low on the approach to land. This was particularly the case when making a carrier or a dummy deck landing approach, when the aimed-for final approach speed had to be more precise and closer to the stall than that required for airfield landings. A torque stall occurs when power is applied at a speed low enough for the engine power transmitted, through the propeller, to overcome the aileron and rudder force available and the aircraft then rotates about the propeller. I never witnessed a torque-stall accident, but it was ably demonstrated and practised at a safe height.

The first three-point landing ashore was not difficult and the landing run was straightforward, provided that one took pains to ensure that the tailwheel was locked and that

Above: The writer, as a Commissioned Pilot, poses in front of Sea Fury VX670 ('124-CW') at RNAS Culdrose while a student on K3 Course.

Left: Everything down for carrier finals, as Sea Fury VW553 ('152') of 804 Squadron, on DLQ, approaches HMS *Vengeance*'s round-down, 1952. The Squadron crest is borne on the tailfin, though no identifying code letter. Notice that the last numeral of the call-sign is carried on the main undercarriage door—an aid to the handling crews.

a trickle of power was used to keep rudder control. A roller landing was equally easy provided these two tasks had been carried out and the power was then applied gently and smoothly. A sudden burst of power, however, could induce a ground loop.

We quickly became attached to the Hawker Sea Fury and moved on to the applied Combat and Tactical part of the course both for air-to-air and ground attack, as there was much to learn and apply. The K3 course had many instructors with wartime and operational experience, well prepared to pass on their knowledge. We and everyone else on the course were like sponges, soaking up as much as we could. Having satisfactorily completed the Weapons and Tactics phase we moved on to Deck Landing Qualification on board HMS Vengeance. On completion, we were appointed to 804 Squadron, in Malta, destined for HMS Glory in the Mediterranean. Our Commanding Officer, Lieutenant Commander J. S. ('Bill') Bailey, was one of the Navy's most experienced pilots and also a qualified test pilot. With his squadron at full strength—twenty-two Sea Furies, maintenance men, and pilots of varying degrees of experience—he was keen to meld us together as a team to achieve our full potential. This he did, both on the 'sports field' (flight deck for deck hockey and lift well for volleyball) and in the air.

The Sea Fury performed well, had a high rate of serviceability and was admired by pilots and maintenance men alike. The flying controls were well harmonised and precise, allowing the pilot to point and aim air-to-ground and air-to-air weapons with great accuracy. As a carrier-based aircraft, perhaps 804 Squadron's achievement, during the Korean War, of 1,000 accident-free deck landings speaks for itself.

Left: Armed with four 60-pound R/Ps, an 804 Squadron Sea Fury, WJ283, crosses the lowered safety barriers as the pilot makes a free take-off from the flight deck of a light fleet carrier.

Below: HMS Glory leaves Grand Harbour, Malta, having taken on her air group, March 1951. Six of 804 Squadron's Sea Furies are visible, and three Fireflies from 812 Squadron are ranged aft. Weeks later, the aircraft would be in action over Korea.

Mediterranean Bale-Out *Lieutenant-Commander Robert McCandless* DSC

On 31 January 1952 I was flying from HMS *Indomitable* in the western Mediterranean as a Lieutenant pilot in 801 Squadron (Sea Fury Mk 11). It was a beautiful day with clear skies and very little wind. My Section Leader, Robin Trelawney, and I were flying CAP over the ship at about 20,000 feet and the Fireflies were playing the part of attacking bombers so that the ship's aircraft direction teams could get some practice. On their instructions we set off to intercept. In due course—Tally Ho! and we positioned ourselves to attack.

Robin turned in on his curve of pursuit and I gave him a few seconds' start before I opened my throttle and turned in on my attack, my leader disappearing under the nose of my aircraft. Unbeknownst to me, however, Robin had throttled back so that he could get a good long camera attack and, unfortunately, our curves of pursuit coincided a couple of hundred yards behind the Firefly. At this point, I was (relatively speaking) above and ahead of my leader and, as we collided, my tail unit struck Robin's starboard wing. He saw that the leading edge of his wing was damaged, but as he was still fully in control of his aircraft he decided that a high-speed landing at North Front, Gibraltar, was a better bet for a safe landing, and so it proved.

For my part, I found myself in a fairly fast spin without any idea what had happened. Normal recovery techniques had no effect, so I decided to abandon the aircraft. Off went the hood and I released the seat straps. I put my hands up to the top of the windscreen to pull myself up and *whoosh*—my right hand had got into the slipstream and my arm was blown right back over my shoulder and along the fuselage, pulling my head out into the slipstream as well. At that point I found that something on my lifejacket had snagged in the cockpit and I was held firmly in this spreadeagled position by the slipstream. I managed to get my heels on to the edge of the bucket seat and pushed and pushed until something gave way and I shot out of the cockpit. The parachute opened and I sat there, floating down gently, and watched my aircraft splash into the water. I saw one of the Fireflies coming round and thought that that was a good thing because at least two other people knew of my problems.

The drill was (and probably still is) that we should release the parachute harness just as our feet hit the water, so I tried to turn the release disc, ready to whack it as entered the water, but I found my right arm painfully reluctant to do as it was told, and by the time this had registered in my somewhat disorientated brain I was in the water and the parachute was settling nicely on top of me. I started to sink and tried to release the parachute harness with my left hand, but no joy. So I decided to inflate my lifejacket to try to keep my head above water. I struggled out from beneath the canopy and it immediately started to sink beside me. My legs were beginning to get entangled with the shroud lines and my lifejacket was not coping with the additional weight of the waterlogged parachute and folded dinghy. I said to myself, 'How bloody stupid to get this far and then drown!'

I reached for the emergency knife to cut through the harness and free myself, and that was when I found out what had snagged in the cockpit. The knife must have caught under the hood rail and held me there until my frantic pushing broke it and set me free—so I had no knife! I then curled up into as small a ball as I could and tried to use both hands to release the harness, but of course it was all so very much tighter because of my inflated lifejacket and because my right hand was not at its best. After another frantic effort it released and the parachute sank like a stone with the harness, but for some reason the dinghy did not come free from the harness and there I was, with my nose just above the water and the full weight of the safety equipment still attached to my lifejacket by the lanyard. Very reluctantly, I released the lanyard, and so my dinghy sank as well. I blew the lifejacket up fully and then lay back, thinking that my right shoulder was bloody painful. The Fireflies stayed with me for quite a long time; in fact, I think they must have stayed long enough to guide the planeguard destroyer, HMS *Battleaxe*, to my position.

The sea was very calm and I could see for some distance. My first indication of rescue was a pall of black smoke on the horizon which kept growing. Next I could see the bow of a ship coming straight towards me, but I began to panic, thinking that they might not see me and not be able to stop in time: there were two enormous bow waves, giving me a very clear indication of fast she was going. However, I was spotted and the ship stopped about a hundred yards away. She lowered her sea boat, which was rowed over to my position—all very efficient. The boat's crew started to lift me into the boat using my right arm with the injured shoulder, but after I had spoken to them quietly in the Naval vernacular I was dropped back into the 'oggin. They then started again using my lifejacket instead of my arms and all went well.

I must have been pretty much in shock by this time because I do not remember being taken into the destroyer. I awoke to feel myself being bumped around and with much bad language assailing my ears. I was lying on a stretcher and the ratings were trying to manœuvre me out through a narrow door into a narrow passage with no chance of succeeding. They had failed to realise that I had awakened and were much surprised when I got off the stretcher, let them get out into the passage and then stepped back on again!

Back on board the carrier I was not particularly popular with those in authority, and I was left in the Sick Bay until it was decided what should be done with me. The 'young Doc' said he was going to reset my shoulder and was going to give me an injection of pentathol (I think) to knock me out while he did the job. He asked me to begin counting. He had expected me to reach about ten before I passed out. I got to ten, then twenty, and then thirty . . . He was beginning to sweat, wondering whether to stop and try again another time. In the event, he continued and when I reached sixty-four, I said to him. 'You callous bastard!' and passed out.

The Board of Inquiry chastised me for 'over-enthusiasm' but did not give me an official reprimand and said that a court-martial would serve no purpose. I went back first to RNH Haslar, where I was told that, by using my arm while it was dislocated, the nerve to the deltoid muscle had been damaged and the muscle was now paralysed. However, they expected it to be a temporary disablement and sent me to Osborne House on the Isle of Wight to recuperate. At that time, the House was a rest home for retired senior civil servants and serving officers. I went from Haslar with another Lieutenant, a seaman officer, and we brought the average age down to about 70! The nurses, an absolutely delightful group of young ladies, seemed to be pleased to see us, and we had a most pleasant sojourn even though my physiotherapy seemed to consist entirely of sawing wood! However, it worked to everybody's satisfaction and I got back to flying nine weeks later.

Below: 801 Squadron's Sea Furies ashore at RNAS Lee-on-Solent, with the Firebrands of 813 Squadron ranged behind them. The tail code letter 'A' identified aircraft attached to HMS *Indomitable*, which implies a date for the photograph of spring 1952. 801 came rather later than other front-line units to the Sea Fury; on the other hand, the Squadron had hitherto been flying the superlative Sea Hornet!

SEA FURY

A Wonderful Experience *Lieutenant Bob Neill*

I was just one of about 250 Royal Navy aircrew who were trained during the years 1950-1954, and I was fortunate enough to enjoy 122 hours of flying the Sea Fury—an aircraft with which I always felt completely at home. She was a superb machine in every respect, particularly in the way she 'talked' to you.

In fact, 1954 was a very good year for me. I was awarded my Wings in February by Admiral Casper John at RAF Syerston, and I had flown the one aircraft that I had joined the Navy to fly—the Seafire 17. This was the only Spitfire that I thought I had a reasonable chance of flying: during the war I just knew I had to do this, and as a seventeen-year-old I realised that only the Royal Navy would have significant numbers flying. During my three months at HMS *Heron* I also met the girl who was to become my wife. I was soon to fly a Sea Fury; indeed I flew twenty-two of them—and all were delightful.

In April of that year I visited RNAS Bramcote to be interviewed by Commander Bertie Vigrass (then CO of the Midland Air Division of the RNVR) as my generation of fighter pilots were to complete our Operational Flying Training with the squadrons we would join at the end of the two-year National Service period. My Midshipman's Journal recorded that 'BWV' thought that the Squadron, having only in February replaced its Seafire 47s with Sea Furies, might become an all-weather fighter unit with Sea Hornets (only recently he denied all knowledge of this!) but that, definitely, we would be flying jets in 1955.

I joined 1833 Squadron in June with two other members of 35 Course, Hamish Lyon-Brown and Tom Holt-Wilson. I was checked out by Lieutenant-Commander Jimmy Maddox, the Division's CFI, after a twenty-minute familiarisation in the T.20, and went solo immediately afterwards in VZ351. Like everyone else I have ever spoken to, I felt completely at home in this wonderful aircraft, and without doubt she was always my favourite. I was just twenty years and four months old, with 250 hours of Prentice, Harvard, Firefly trainer and Seafire flying, and, for me, life could not be better.

Fam II was the next day in F.B.11 VW656, and I began to enjoy the Ultimate Piston Fighter with those superb ailerons (which must surely have been the best ever on a non-powered system). Fam III and Fam IV did not seem to happen on 1833 Squadron, and by the end of the month I had almost twenty hours on type. After only five I was detailed to take our Squadron CO, Lieutenant-Commander David Jenkins, in a T.20 back to RNAS Ford on a beautiful

Below: A line-up of Sea Furies of 1833 Squadron at Bramcote in 1954; the first three aircraft are T.20 trainers and the remainder single-seat F.B.11s. Leaving aside the variable qualities of the Supermarine Attacker, the Sea Fury was the fastest and most powerful aircraft to serve with the Royal Naval Volunteer Reserve.

Above: A trio of Sea Fury Mk 11s up from Bramcote. The RNVR aircraft were finished and marked in identical fashion to those in the front-line Fleet Air Arm squadrons. Notice the little stripe across the wing-root fillet, indicating the position of the pull-down access footstep beneath.

Sunday evening (COs were collected from and returned to their nearest naval air station each weekend). David was a splendid CO and did not mind a bit being flown by a very low-hour driver—at least, he did not say so! The icing on the cake was the trip back—high speed and low level. A book was kept on the best times!

We had a very active CBGLO (Carrier-Borne Ground Liaison Officer) attached to the MAD who organised many army co-operation exercises. I well remember 'attacking' troops dug in near Aldershot and passing very close to an Air India Constellation, wheels and flaps down, on a long final into Heathrow. No 'air miss' was ever reported so we lived to fly another day! We flew many interception exercises with RAF Hack Green, our dummy dives were assessed, battle formations were practised, and camera gun firing results were recorded by Wrens. We flew in Exercise 'Dividend' in July and 33 hours were chalked up that month.

In September the Squadron had its two-week annual training at RNAS Hal Far. This was my first time away from Britain and I could not believe how hot it was. We flew intensively from 0700 to 1300 every day, firing R/Ps, dropping practice bombs and doing some air-to-air firing against winged targets towed by Sturgeons operated by 728 Squadron. I didn't find them very easy to hit. Off-duty time was spent enjoying the many delights that Malta had to offer.

The culmination of 35 Course's training was our Deck Landing and Armament Camp at Yeovilton, where Admiral Commanding Reserves, or his staff, formed 'X' Squadron, commanded by Lieutenant-Commander Maurice Birrell with Lieutenant Harry Burman as 'Bats'. We joined with aircraft borrowed from our Divisions. There were eleven of us and we all completed some eighty ADDLS before going to HMS *Illustrious*, which was steaming 27 nautical miles south-west of Portland Bill. I flew out as Number Two to Maurice. We saw the ship—how tiny she looked! 'MB' landed on, I flew my circuit to get the feel of things and to take the pre-arranged wave off. I duly completed six landings that afternoon. No one forgets his first DL, and although Johnny Treloar, *Illustrious*'s own batsman, did not like the low 'cuts' that we had been used to, I was able to adjust to his style. I shall always remember, on my first arrival, looking to port, seeing the sea rushing past and experiencing instant panic as I thought my Sea Fury was still moving and would trundle over the bow. I squeezed the brake lever but to no effect—since, of course, I had in fact stopped. Push back, free take-off, and five more landings all went more or less according to plan. An order to report to Commander Air had me worried, but he was kind enough to say, 'Well done!' Most of my colleagues were not so happy with the change in batting styles, so next day we all completed another ADDL session in 'JT' style. The next day it was back to the ship to complete my ten. Many difficulties remained, however, and the crew room 'scoreboard' read 49 for 8. The eight accidents, or incidents, included Alan Braithwaite who got really low and slow and torque-stalled astern of the carrier in his Firefly Mk 6, but he got out before it sank to the bottom of Lyme Bay

I remember singing to myself, 'Ole! I am a bandit!' (a popular song of the time) as I flew the circuit, so I must have been relatively relaxed in my Fury. Ninety-two knots was the correct final approach speed, a slight tremor through the stick indicating that a touch more throttle was needed; it was easy to add the right amount with the smooth, progressive throttle control lever. Nevertheless, none of us could understand why we had two batsmen with such different ideas as to how it should be done!

DLs completed, and National Service over. It was for me a wonderful experience—perhaps, indeed, the making of me. I went on to fly the Sea Fury for another nine months. I then moved into the jet era, flying the unloved Attacker—quite another story, however!

Below: An RNVR Sea Fury, WG625 of 1831 Squadron, meets HMS *Illustrious*'s barrier after bouncing over the wires during Deck Landing Training, July 1954. The pilot, Sub-Lieutenant Jones, was unscathed.

FROM THE COCKPIT

The Colour of Adrenalin *Lieutenant-Commander Peter Sheppard* AFC

I did my flying training in 1952 down at Culdrose, as was the norm. In fact, it appears that I, along with six of my colleagues, was 'creamed off' from my course (25 students) on Seafires (which I was thoroughly enjoying, by the way), earmarked for Meteor flying at Culdrose with a view to moving on to the first Attacker squadron. The problem for me was that I wanted to go to Korea, and it was very evident that the jet squadrons were not going there. My old boxing instructor had been killed out there, and I was determined to avenge his death. Luckily Commander (Air), Freddie Stovin-Bradford, happened to be an old boy from my school (and, by the way, a wonderful pianist). I was enjoying the Meteor, but his advice was that I was not doing particularly well on it and that I should go and fly the Sea Fury. I went away clutching the Pilot's Notes, did a few 'famils' and was hooked. That was in November 1952, and it marked the beginning of a love affair.

I was a late entrant into the Korean War. I was due to go to *Ocean*, but first there was some deck-landing practice in HMS *Triumph* to be carried out. I made twenty-seven deck landings during DLP, all but two of which were performed following free take-offs. In March 1953 we went out to Hal Far and began flying together as a squadron (807) while *Ocean* was in refit prior to accepting us as an operational squadron. We had the chance to do some refresher DLP in *Indomitable*, and it was here that my first experience of the catapult ended somewhat ignominiously. I was in position, running the engine up to full power and with my hand raised to indicate that I was ready, the launch officer waving his green flag and the green light on Flyco lit up—when the hold-back ring broke. I therefore found myself moving down the catapult, but not very quickly, and I ended up trickling over the bow and into the briny. I had been a champion swimmer at school and so, realising that the aircraft was on top of me, I swam out of the cockpit and downwards as far as I could, whereupon I turned and swam as fast as I could away from the ship, which of course was bearing down on the spot where my aircraft had hit the water. I popped to the surface after about a minute, expecting to be well clear of everything, but to my consternation discovered that I was a mere foot away from the sinking Sea Fury's fuselage. In fact, the interval that elapsed between the impact of the aircraft and the appearance of my head bobbing about had been meticulously timed up above, on board ship, as nine seconds. Time certainly does fly when you're enjoying yourself! Back on board ship, I was liberally laced—and night flying was scheduled that evening!

So off we went to Korea. There I had my first taste of 'triple-A', which looked very pretty and did not cause many problems until one day we ran into a box barrage. We were tasked with bombing a railway yard at the time, and one of our number—nameless, of course—immediately pulled up and high-tailed it away out of danger. I pulled up but stalled my Fury and went straight back into the box!

We sometimes carried a drop tank modified to act as a photographic pack, and it fell to me one day, as junior member of the Squadron, to act as tail-end Charlie and take this pack aloft. The idea was that I would snap the first three Furies as they attacked their target, follow down and drop my bombs and then immediately switch to the rear camera and photograph the damage caused by my own bombs bursting. The tactic left the fourth aircraft somewhat short of fuel, and now, flying back to the ship, I was informed that the carrier was in fog. This normally meant that I would have to fly back to recover on the mainland, but in the event it was decided to give me a carrier-controlled approach—something I had never actually rehearsed (and neither had the ship). Trusting to beginner's luck, therefore, I went towards the ship obeying all the radar instructions, slowing to landing speed and with everything dangling as appropriate, only to get a glimpse of a carrier island at right angles to what should have been my correct line of approach. I tried another approach, but this time was informed that I had been heard, had flown close by the bows and was now off to starboard, whereupon I was advised to ditch. By this time I was running on empty, but I knew that there were sharks around and the idea of a dunking held little appeal. I wondered how close I might be able to get to the attendant destroyer if I went into the sea, and was told that she was out of view because of the fog. However, just as I was contemplating the advantages of crashing gently into something more solid that the Yellow Sea in order to attract the attention of my rescuers, a gap appeared in the fog and I found myself close to the deck and so I plonked the aircraft down off a right-hand turn—absolutely against the rules because, for one thing, an overshoot could induce the dreaded torque stall—and, luckily, caught a wire. I had ninety seconds' flying fuel left. I duly pressed the R/T button: 'Thank you, God!'

On another occasion I was flying with a Dutch pilot as wingman. This was the time of the truce, and the rules stated that we were forbidden to fly within three miles of the coast of Korea, but he had spotted a Royal Netherlands Navy ship below, dressed overall in commemoration of Queen Juliana's birthday. Down we went, beating merry hell out of the vessel, flying between the masts and the rigging and generally alarming all on board. It was great fun, but we suddenly got a voice on the radio saying, 'Report to your mother ship!' Having thus been sent back with our tails between our legs, we reported to the Captain when back on board, whereupon we were told that we were confined to cabin and would be flown back home for court martial—breaking the rules of the truce could restart the war! Luckily I had a splendid CO, who advised the Captain that he needed to take Sheppard flying before he went back to Britain. He led me to precisely the same spot where our fun and games had taken place the previous day, and on our return the CO informed the Captain that in fact we had been just outside the three-mile exclusion and that the ship had been slightly out of the position stated. Sheppard and his Dutch companion had wriggled free!

Stories concerning RATOG abound. One day we needed to take off but the catapult was not working and there was no wind to speak of. Thus rocket assistance was the solu-

Left: RATOG take-offs were fraught but unfailingly impressive spectacles. Here, abreast *Ocean*'s island and slightly off the centreline, the pilot of Sea Fury '159'—from 807 Squadron—has just pressed the button.
Below, left and right: Barrier encounters for two 807 Squadron Furies while landing on board HMS *Ocean*—an unidentified aircraft at left and WM488 at right.

tion. Sadly, we quickly lost a Firefly when the aircraft was launched but only one side of the RATOG fitting fired successfully. The aircraft went over the side upside down and one of the crewmen was drowned. Such departures were always somewhat fraught: if the rockets were fired a fraction early or a fraction late, the full benefit of the system could not be utilised. We had already practised these assisted take-offs during training, albeit ashore, and we were all well briefed on the procedure—all of us except three Dutchmen who were on the Squadron. One went off but fired the rockets a touch early or a touch late and, as a result, went straight into the water off the bow. He was quickly picked up by the SAR helicopter and deposited safely back on board. The second chap, the senior Dutch pilot, went off but fired a fraction late. We all waited for the big splash ahead of the ship but nothing happened and eventually the Sea Fury appeared in the distance, having scraped the wavetops before managing to get airborne. The immortal words, heavily accented, came over the radio: 'This is —— dangerous!' In a novel procedure, we also used RATOG during our Coronation flypast. We were in harbour at the time, and so the ship was swung on her anchor so that she was pointing in a safe direction before we were all launched in succession, and thankfully without incident.

My twenty-first birthday in October 1953 was an occasion that somewhat coloured my later career. We were due to go flying quite early the following morning, so I decided that I would not declare myself, since this was the date on which one was expected to purchase copious amounts of liquid refreshment for one's squadron mates:

I would do so one day late. Unfortunately one of my friends, with whom I had been on the course, came into the bar and proclaimed loudly, 'Ah Sheppard—happy birthday! Twenty-first, isn't it?' This of course was the signal for everybody to join in. I remember absolutely nothing at all about the remainder of the evening but a complete blur, my next recollection being the flying the following day. I was tail-end Charlie of four, and I recall that each of the three, when landing-on, tipped his nose into the barrier. My own landing, the last of the four, was, ironically, quite perfect, but I nevertheless heard the words over the tannoy, 'Sub-Lieutenant Sheppard—report to the bridge.' I suddenly thought that I was perhaps going to be congratulated for my peerless landing, but instead the Captain directed me to Flyco and my CO. No pat on the back was forthcoming, however, as it was explained to me that the Commander had been on a witch-hunt, which meant that he had looked at my wine bill for the previous evening—ninety-seven spirits, twelve pints of beer and four bottles of wine, although not, as I remarked to the CO, all consumed by myself—and was demanding punishment. The considered judgement of my excellent CO, Lieutenant-Commander Laurie Brander, was that, in recompense for my misdeeds, I had to 'spend at least the same amount again tonight'. Another one that I got away with!

After that little episode I did not have much more to do with the Fury—which was coming to the end of its front-line career—until about 1972, when RNAS Yeovilton was given an aircraft by Hawker on condition that the Navy would refurbish it and maintain it in flying condition. I was at

FROM THE COCKPIT

Left: Sea Fury TF956—the very first Mk 11 to be produced and a Korean War veteran—was the founder member of the the RN Historic Flight and the aircraft that the writer flew in many displays up and down the country. It is seen here prior to its career as a demonstration aircraft. The elliptical fairing on the main undercarriage door is not an original design feature.
Overleaf: The same aircraft in the Heron Flight hangar in 1971, its refurbishment almost complete.

Yeovilton having just completed my 'famils' in the Phantom, when the Sea Fury was wheeled out ready for its first test flight after it rejuvenation. Duncan Simpson, the Hawker Chief Test Pilot, had carried out a trip and then he had handed the aircraft over to the Navy. I was nominated to conduct further flight testing since after casting around for a suitable pilot someone had observed that I was the chap required, on the strength of my having flown the aircraft twenty years before. I therefore carried out a 'famil'—having, only two hours earlier, been flying a Mach 2 Phantom—and the indelible memory etched in the mind is that whereas the cows at the end of Yeovilton's runway had taken no notice as the big jet roared all over the place, the first approach by the Sea Fury sent them scattering in all directions! My second flight was the first 'official' flight, and I was able to put the aircraft truly through its paces. Thus began my career as the RN Sea Fury display pilot—and in time I notched up more hours in the aircraft in this way than I had accumulated on operational duties. This was also the beginning of what came to be know as the Royal Naval Historic Flight, so well known nowadays at public flying displays.

I have a plethora of stories about flying and displaying the Fury—some of them for adult reading only! I loved the aircraft: I was never very accomplished in competitive aerobatics, which frequently involves a lot of sudden, sharp manœuvres, but I thoroughly enjoyed speeding around in this wonderful aeroplane. Back in the early 1970s the limitations on display flying were far less restrictive than they are today, and I was in the enviable position of being able to write my own script for the displays I was performing, subject only to the approval of the admirals. I knew that the 'g' limit was somewhere about 10 or 12 (it was a strong aeroplane) and therefore worked within the constraints of +5g and -3g. One of the things that I discovered while at Hal Far and waiting to go to Korea was that you could actually pull 12g in a Fury. This came about because on one occasion, during armament practice, I had dropped the wrong bomb at the wrong time. I had caused a number of rivets to pop, but it was an immensely strong aeroplane and it had held. The essential parameters were that the aeros had to be kept flowing, fairly tight, and within sight of the crowd below. However, it was impossible to display in this way for more than about five minutes without repeating a manœuvre that had already been carried out (to the detriment, of course, of spectator interest).

Pilots were not allowed to perform at Farnborough without carrying out a rehearsal on site, and one memorable year I was about to take off from Yeovilton to carry out the practice when it was discovered that a swarm of bees had settled in the aircraft's tailplane. It was quite late in the evening, but we managed to find someone to deal with the problem, whereupon I set off. I arrived at Farnborough and went through the programme. However, at one point in the proceedings I was upside down in the middle of a four-point roll at fairly low level when the one and only bee to have survived the cleansing of the aircraft decided to take a trip round the cockpit. The aircraft's ensuing manœuvres were unscheduled, interesting and difficult to explain to the onlookers!

A completely separate assignment one day involved the retrieval of ex-German Sea Furies and their recovery for a friend at Blackbushe, who wanted to refurbish and repaint these bright red two-seaters that had hitherto been used for target-towing. One day I was asked to do a display in one of these newly acquired aircraft in front of a Sunday market. One manœuvre that could be performed when flying a two-seat Fury but forbidden in a single-seater was a deliberate spin. A torque stall could be induced at a safe height, the aircraft being recoverable by means of a quick flick roll, and indeed I had put this into the display on several occasions. On one occasion, however, I asked too much of the aircraft: I got over the top at about 2,500 feet but when I pushed the aircraft went into an inverted spin. It took me a moment to realise what was happening, Down to 2,000 feet, I picked out a field far away from the crowd, but thankfully I managed to land conventionally, having, along the way discovered the colour of adrenalin. I was met by the owner of the airfield, who opined that the display had been 'flippin' marvellous'! I had got away with it once more—but I never included that particular aero in my repertoire again!

An interesting aspect of the German Sea Fury story is that before being delivered to Blackbushe the returning aircraft had to call in at Heathrow in order to clear customs. One of the aircraft happened to stay there as it was being converted to a single-seater and being resprayed, and thus required a test flight before it could be handed over to its new owners. I went to Heathrow to conduct the

COURTESY GEOFF WAKEHAM

DANGER
UNAUTHORISED
PERSONS
KEEP OUT

flight and was instructed to take off, fly around for half and hour and then land back, being advised to call the ATC in the way of a regular airliner. I had to explain that all I had a rather primitive radio—oh, and a compass. Well, said ATC, there are two runways at Heathrow, and can you see that airliner on your left? Yes? And can you formate on him and land on the runway to the right? I have often wondered what the passengers thought as they prepared for their touchdown!

Flying Yeovilton's Sea Fury was a privilege that brought with it many wonderful experiences. Once I was interviewed having been, for a change, flying the Navy's Swordfish during a display. The interviewer, sure that he already knew the answer, invited me to give the name of my favourite aircraft, and was surprised to hear a two-word rejoinder instead of one word. 'The Sea Fury? Rather than the Swordfish?' was the incredulous response. 'Well, for one thing, you can fly the Sea Fury upside down,' I countered. 'Upside down? Why is that?' 'Well, it takes the weight off your "parts",' I said in jest, 'but edit that bit out of the interview, of course!' The recording duly went out, unabridged, and my comment was committed to posterity (and, no doubt believed by some). I was more discreet thereafter!

I have had the pleasure of formating with Concorde and formating with the Red Arrows (during the Gnat era); at the other end of the scale I have accompanied motorised gliders in the Sea Fury. Finally, I am thankful to those in higher office who resisted promoting me (which would have put me behind a desk) in order to keep me flying this wonderful aircraft—although, admittedly, the additional pension would have been handy in these days of retirement!

Above: TF956 in sparkling finish in its full display livery. Sadly, the aircraft was lost in 1989 when, as a result of an undercarriage failure, it had to be ditched in the Clyde following a display at Prestwick. The pilot, John Beattie, baled out and was rescued.
Below: TF956's place was taken by Mk 11 VR930, which was already acting as a source of spares for the RNHF. It joined the display circuit in 2001.

FROM THE COCKPIT

Fate Takes a Hand *Sub-Lieutenant Peter Rainbird* CBE DL

As the age of eighteen approached, it was a certainty that I would have to do National Service—as indeed every male of my age would be obliged to do provided he were in good health. How I arrived at joining the Fleet Air Arm is still a bit of a mystery as my father had served in the Essex Yeomanry and I was prominent in the Army section of the CCF at school. Moreover, living in Essex, where the Army was embedded in the county's culture, it looked as though I was destined to become a 'pongo'. The accepted form in my circle would to have been to obtain a commission and then engineer, with the help of those better connected (i.e., the Colonel), a posting to Orsett Camp for the remainder of one's service, during which time it would be hunting twice a week in the season.

But fate took a hand, as it usually does, when a colleague at school showed me an advertisement in *Flight* magazine seeking recruits to become aircrew in the Navy. I clearly remember him saying, 'Look at the uniforms', and undoubtedly this was a factor, if not the major factor, in my ultimate decision. Interestingly, one of the figures in the advertisement was Lieutenant-Commander John David, whom I was to come across later during my time.

More seriously, living almost midway between the RAF stations at Hornchurch and North Weald throughout World War II, I was witness to constant activity in the air and became very proficient in aircraft recognition. However, I cannot remember that it ever crossed my mind to join the RAF, although I was aware of the Fleet Air Arm's exploits, including the Battle of Taranto. Later, two school friends applied and gained entry to the Royal Naval College at Dartmouth, which no doubt further influenced my decision.

Thus I applied, and was successful, and in due course I found myself at RNAS Lee-on-Solent (HMS *Dædalus*) on 3 November 1952 as a Naval Airman 2nd Class to begin what was to become, for the next four years, an adventure which embraced great excitement and joy, fear and sadness and, above all, camaraderie. There followed basic training at *Dædalus* and on board HMS *Indefatigable*, pre-flight training at RNAS Gosport (HMS *Siskin*) now as a Temporary Acting Midshipman (A) RNVR and finally, in May 1953, a spell at RAF Syerston to begin flying training on Prentices and then Harvards. I proudly received my Wings from Rear-Admiral Caspar John in February 1954 and was then posted, together with those of my colleagues who had been selected to become fighter pilots, to 764 Squadron at RNAS Yeovilton (HMS *Heron*) to begin operational training on Seafire 17s.

The Fleet Air Arm was in major transition at about this time. The Korean War had finished in early 1953. From early 1951 the Hawker Sea Fury, that great and much underrated aeroplane, and which had acquitted itself so brilliantly in the Korean War, was giving way to the Navy's first jet fighter, the Supermarine Attacker F.1, a controversial aircraft which, as could be seen in hindsight, was little more than a stop-gap. In turn the Attacker was giving way to a second-generation jet fighter, the Hawker Sea Hawk—an infinitely more likeable aeroplane. Nevertheless, this was progress, if a little late when measured against that in the US Navy, which had introduced its first carrier-borne jet aircraft during the Korean conflict and in doing so gained invaluable combat experience and decisively overtook the pioneering work that the Royal Navy had carried out in the late 1940s.

The light fleet carriers *Albion*, *Centaur* and *Bulwark* were coming on stream, originally to the then conventional designs but quickly upgraded to include the latest British inventions, the angled deck, the mirror landing sight and the steam catapult—inventions that revolutionised carrier operations and in updated forms exist to this day. Nationally, also, things were difficult: it was a very few years since the end of the war, rationing had only just ended, and the country was still deeply in debt.

It was against this backcloth that I and my colleagues came to do our National Service. These enormous changes in military aviation, however, did not consciously impact on us—I am sure we did not recognise them at the time—until we had completed Operational Flying School Part I on 764 Squadron. I believe that we were the second or third from last course to fly the Seafire 17 in training: henceforth pilots successfully completing their flying training at Syerston were to go to RAF Valley and complete OFS I on the Vampire and then to RNAS Lossiemouth for OFS II on the Sea Hawk. In this uncertain environment, at the end May 1954, OFS II for piston-engine pilots therefore no longer existed. However, as we were obliged to do two years' service on the Reserve, someone had the bright idea of farming us out to the RNVR air divisions to which we would be assigned after we had completed National Service.

I and three colleagues were destined to join the Southern Air Division RNVR at RAF Benson, where there were two squadrons, 1832 and 1836 (formerly 1832A); a third, 1834, was based at Yeovilton, and all three were equipped with the Sea Fury F.B.11. It fell to us to join 1834, commanded by Lieutenant-Commander Tony Ford. So we remained at Yeovilton, although the pattern of our lives changed quite dramatically as, being a Reserve, the Squadron operated at weekends and on Bank Holidays and we therefore had to take our 'weekends' during the week, usually on Monday and Tuesday. We were assigned a mature RN Lieutenant, Harry Burman, a qualified Deck Landing Officer, as our mentor and guide, and it was under his direction that we began flying this wonderful aeroplane.

This was a 'one-off' situation born of expediency. It was not, nor was it intended to be, an OFS II. However, there was plenty of flying with experienced pilots, which undoubtedly aided our progress. It was during this period, when landing a Sea Fury T.20 on Runway 27 in a crosswind, that I scraped the port wing on its surface—a legacy I am not particularly proud of although I plead fewer than fifteen hours on type at the time!

It was on 1 September 1954 that we became a self-contained albeit temporary unit known as X Squadron. We were no longer attached to a weekend outfit and returned to a normal working week. We were reunited with our friends, who had also been farmed out as we were following our time with 764, and we were joined by those (three in number) who had gone down the anti-submarine route and were now flying the Firefly. We hadn't seen them since they received their Wings at Syerston. Our aeroplanes were supplied by the various RNVR Air Divisions to which we had been attached. Our CO was Lieutenant-Commander Maurice Birrell, who was filling in time as he waited to take command of 891 Squadron, the third front-line unit to be re-forming at Yeovilton with the Navy's new all-weather fighter, the Sea Venom. Harry Burman remained with us, and we were provided with our own AEO.

Although we were due to be demobbed in mid-October, a mere six weeks ahead, there then began what was probably the most intensive period of our careers so far, concentrating on weapons training and ADDLS, the former at Treligga Range in Cornwall. HMS *Illustrious*, that grand old lady of World War II, which was concluding its commission as the Navy's deck-landing training carrier, was booked for us to 'go to the deck' for the first time, for three days commencing on Monday 4 October. This was to be a fitting conclusion to National Service and, although not without incident, very satisfying for those of us who survived unscathed.

The Sea Fury appears much more in my log book than the seven other types that I was privileged to fly, and it was undoubtedly the most rewarding, although, by the time I flew one, it was very much yesterday's aeroplane—at least as far as the Navy was concerned. Although not designed originally for carrier operations, it must rank as one of the best of the regrettably few successful British-built aeroplanes to become so. It was powerful, stable and solid in flight, highly manœuvrable and, if respected, not difficult to land, both on land and at sea. However, it was not without vices. Whereas with the Seafire there was a measure of control below the stall which could be welcome when landing, the Sea Fury had a tendency the other way in similar circumstances. I was comfortable during the few deck landings I carried out in the Sea Fury, but I was very aware that accuracy on the approach was vital with regard to speed, attitude, height and power. With an engine of 2,600hp out front, it was vital, when landing on, not to get too low and slow because the only response was to apply power, almost certainly in a panic and almost certainly resulting in a torque stall and landing upside down in the sea—clearly, not what was intended. We were made well aware of this, and the first to go to the deck from X Squadron was a Sub-Lieutenant (A) RNVR in, as it happens, a Firefly and who had been adjudged to have been a model student during ADDLs and would therefore be good for the confidence for those following. Unfortunately it was not to be, and he got low and slow on the approach, inevitably finishing in the sea but happily surviving the experience. Not much of a

Left: The personnel of X Squadron, October 1954: (seated, left to right) John Philips, Pete Stubbings, our AEO, Harry Burman, Maurice Birrell (CO), Bill Coates and Alan Brathwaite; (standing, left to right) Hamish Lyon-Brown, Bill Brennen, Tom Holt-Wilson, Adam Charn-aud, Peter Rainbird, Bob Neill and John Elliot.
Above: Brilliantly illuminated by a setting sun, a pair of Sea Furies from 1834 Squadron formate for the camera.
Right: The writer performs a free take-off from HMS *Illustrious*, 6 October 1954.

confidence booster! The torque stall was characteristic of powerful single-engine piston aircraft of the 1940s and early 1950s though was not of particular significance on land. However, it was of special relevance to carrier-borne aircraft because of the very narrow limitations when landing-on.

I believe that the members of X Squadron may have been the last pilots to land the Sea Fury on a carrier as *Illustrious* was due to be paid off before the end of that year, and I am not aware that courses of National Service pilots following us went to the deck at all. Indeed, there were already signs that opportunities to do National Service in the Fleet Air Arm were coming to an end.

I referred earlier to the circumstances in which I and my colleagues came to do our National Service. I do not think we were aware when we were recruited that the Admiralty needed to be assured that a flow of trained pilots would be available should the war in Korea not come to a speedy conclusion. As is now known, it did end in early 1953, leading, I suspect, to a reappraisal of defence needs against a background of national indebtedness and the measures required to tackle this. Unwittingly, we were caught up in, and were part of, this time of transition. On reflection, apart from the great privilege of being part of the Fleet Air Arm for a few short years, those years were a period of great change and exposed us to a variety of experiences which would probably not have been available at any other time.

So X Squadron was disbanded in mid-October 1954 and its members went back to civilian life, feeling privileged to have been part of such a great and exciting service. I joined 1836 Squadron at RAF Benson and continued flying the Sea Fury at weekends until March 1956, converting then to the Attacker F.B.2. This was all part of the inevitable changes, and yes, I can say I flew a jet fighter, but for the sheer joy of flying give me the Sea Fury every time.

INTO ACTION

Captain Alan J. Leahy CBE DSC

WHEN I sat in that Sea Fury on that first occasion at RNAS St Merryn it could not have been predicted that, six months later, a war would break out thousands of miles away in the Korean peninsula; still less could it have possibly been imagined that I myself, along with many of my friends and colleagues in the Fleet Air Arm, would be flying the Sea Fury in anger, and intimately involved in that war. Our skills and capabilities, honed by constant practice, would be put to the ultimate test. Five British and Commonwealth carriers would be involved in hostilities over the three years' duration of the war, the Royal Navy's light fleet carriers *Triumph*, *Theseus*, *Ocean* and *Glory* and the Royal Australian Navy carrier *Sydney*. Three principal aircraft types were used to carry the fight, the Seafire, which saw service in the Far East only on board *Triumph* and was withdrawn from front-line service when the carrier's tour finished in September 1950; and the Firefly and the Sea Fury, both of which served on the other four carriers throughout the rest of the war.

On completion of my time as a weapons instructor at Culdrose I was surprised that I did not get appointed to a Squadron; instead, I was appointed to RNAS Lee-on-Solent (HMS *Dædalus*), in charge of the Fleet Air Arm Field Gun Crew, training to take part in the Royal Tournament at Earl's Court. I realise that I was a weapons instructor, but really—field guns! Six months later, however, at the beginning of August 1952, I was at RNAS Hal Far (HMS *Falcon*) and a member of 801 Squadron, working up in preparation for embarking in HMS *Glory*. The carrier had returned to the Mediterranean from Korea with the 14th Carrier Air Group embarked and had been in the floating dry dock during May. Immediately afterwards she embarked 807 and 898

Below: The author as a lieutenant (second from left) during the Korean operations, in company with Lieutenants J. H. Fiddian-Green (far left), P. Wheatley (second from right—Squadron Duty Boy that day and the author's regular wingman) and V. B. Mitchell. The author's oxygen mask and attached helmet are slung over his left shoulder and the three who are in their immersion suits are clasping their knee-pads in their left hands with all the details of the sortie that they are about to fly. The Sea Fury's 20mm magazines are revealed within the port wing.

(Sea Fury) Squadrons and proceeded with the Mediterranean Fleet to Istanbul for a visit. The *coup* in which Colonel Nasser deposed King Farouk, however, cut short the visit before it had even started and the Fleet was moved to where it would be best placed to look after British interests in Egypt, should they be required.

All these excitements did not affect 801 Squadron's preparation to embark in *Glory* at the beginning of September. As the Squadron had not been embarked since March that year, and as many personnel on the Squadron had served their time and had been replaced, there was a lot of work to be done. For the aircrew, the first priority was ADDLs and the second was take-offs. Referring back to the three methods of taking off from the carrier outlined

Right: HMS Glory *during* the Korean operations, with a Sea Fury being readied on the ship's single catapult.
Below: Another photograph of HMS *Glory*, here in the Garden Island Dockyard in Sydney, where she underwent a two-month refit in late 1951 prior to deploying to Korean waters. The two 804 Squadron Furies have their canopies and engine cowlings protected, and the ship's S-51 SAR helicopter (note the US markings) is also on deck.

Left: A Sea Fury of 807 Squadron is moved by lighter en route to or from her carrier. This photograph was taken in the Mediterranean, but the same system was often employed for transferring damaged aircraft in the Korean theatre.
Right: Smoke and flame as an 801 Squadron Fury, on its way to conduct an R/P strike, crosses Glory's safety barriers and its RATOG fires.
Below: RATOG practice at RNAS Hal Far, with plenty of dust to add to the efflux. In the centre foreground, the man standing by the runway has indicated when the pilot should press the button; his companion is either nonchalantly himself lighting up or, more probably, shielding his face from the fast-approaching cloud.

earlier, it should be mentioned that a free take off was a non-starter when the ship has a full suite of aircraft, that the catapult take-off was the preferred method (but the light fleet carriers only had one catapult, and this could go unserviceable), and that RATOG was nobody's favourite but needed to be available as a 'spare' system. In fact, in order to practise RATOG it was necessary to take two aircraft out of the flying programme and fit them up with the take-off rocket mountings. The drill then was for the pilot to line the aircraft up on the runway and, when cleared for take-off, accelerate as fast as possible towards a man standing at the side of the runway with a flag at the position calculated to be that at which the aircraft was on the point of leaving the ground. As the pilot reached the man with the flag he would fire the rockets and the aircraft would leap into the air. At this point was necessary to make sure that the tendency for the aircraft to pitch-up was controlled. Once under full control, the aircraft would fly round into the circuit and land back on the runway with the gear still attached; at sea the gear would be jettisoned. This was not a difficult exercise, but the idea that one of the rockets might take off on its own and leave the pilot with one wing and its rocket trying to reach the stars and the other wing trying desperately to stay on the ground—as indeed happened to a Firefly—was not entirely reassuring.

Other exercises more appropriate to fighting a war also took place, as follows:

Combat Air Patrol (CAP)—Air defence exercises under the control of Malta Radar.

45 Degree Dive Bombing (DB)—In Korea it had been found that flak was rarely present above 3,000–4,000 feet, and so it was possible to roll into the dive from 4,000 feet and pull out of the dive by 1,500—any lower than that and the pilot was vulnerable to fragments from the explosion of his own bomb.

45 Degree (DB) Division Attacks—These attacks were carried out from a shallow echelon with two-second intervals between each aircraft.

45 Degree Rocket Attacks (RP)—While working up ashore it was possible to run RP and DB programmes together, but once embarked it was decided that it was more effective to keep the Sea Furies in the bombing rôle and the Fireflies in the rocketing rôle as a lot of maintenance time was required to adapt each aircraft.

Above: An interesting take-off: Sea Fury '132-O'—probably either WJ246 or WM489—about to leave the carrier *Ocean*, equipped with RATOG that has apparently not been fired, either deliberately or as a result of an error or malfunction. The tailwheel has just risen from the deck, so the pilot was presumably successful in his efforts to become airborne.

Strafing.—All pilots were refreshed in carrying out attacks in 20-degree dives. The opportunity was taken to make good use of towed targets astern of various ships.

Bombardment Spotting.—Pilots were trained in working with ships in order to direct the ships' gunfire against distant targets.

Finally on 2 September 1952, 801 and 821 Squadrons embarked in HMS *Glory*. In the first week most pilots had carried out at least ten launches and recoveries and practised strafing and dive-bombing using towed targets astern of the ship. Interception exercises under the ship's control were carried out against aircraft from Hal Far.

On 11 September the flying programme contained RATOG launches for 801 Squadron. At the briefing it was emphasised that it was important that the RATOG master switch should not be activated until the aircraft was lined up on deck, ready to take off. At one stage the press-to-transmit (PTT) switch was in the end of the throttle twist grip. After everyone had got used to that, a modification moved the RATOG firing button to the throttle twist grip in lieu of the PTT switch. On one occasion, prior to a RATOG launch on board *Ocean*, the leader of a flight of four aircraft called for a radio check. One aircraft leapt out of its chocks and savaged the island in front of it when the pilot mistook the RATOG firing button for the PTT button and, unfortunately, when the rockets fired NA1 R. F. Herbert was killed when blown over the side. Possibly as a result of that accident, the RATOG firing button was moved again, this time to a position immediately above the contacting altimeter, but there was no way in which the pilot could see this new location unless he

ducked his head down to see it tucked under the coaming over the instruments.

When it was my turn to be launched as directed, I went up to full power and when cleared to go took off down the deck to the man who marked the spot where the rockets were to be fired. The briefing had been clear: 'If your rockets do not fire, close the throttle and apply the brakes and you will stop before you reach the end of the deck.' My rockets did not fire, but I did not do as briefed and looked under the coaming to see if I had put my finger in the punkah louvre next to the RATOG firing button by mistake. By the time I reverted to doing what I had been briefed to do, it was too late. My Sea Fury taxied slowly over the bow with the brakes hard on.

Eight years previously, when I was at the US Naval Air Training Base at Pensacola as part of the course before we students qualified for our Wings, we were required to survive the Dilbert Dunker. This was the cockpit section of a SNJ Harvard which sat at the top of a 45-degree ramp. After the student was strapped into a parachute and the pilot's seat to the satisfaction of the instructors, the cockpit section was released and slid down the ramp. Immediately it hit the water it turned upside down. In the water there were two divers who were there to help anyone who failed to get clear of the cockpit on his own.

When my Sea Fury struck the water I could see from the disc of the propeller hitting the sea that we were vertical. When I opened my eyes the cockpit was full of water and bubbles and I started to get out. I released the seat harness and then the parachute harness, and stood up in the cockpit. The speed of the aircraft sinking and turning upside down forced me back against the cockpit hood, which had been open for take-off. On the front of the cockpit hood were two spigots, designed to stop the hood from fluttering at high speed by slotting into the top of the windscreen. However, I was trapped by these spigots sticking into the back of my Mae West and thus I had to get back down into the cockpit and turn round facing the tail so that I could cover the spigots with my hands and then lever myself out using the canopy. Clear of the aircraft, I saw it sinking upside down beside me. All this time I had been waiting for the ship to hit one or the other or both of us.

Now that I was clear of the aircraft I thought that it might be better to stay where I was until the ship

Above: VW565 from 804 Squadron (*Glory*) 'in the drink' as a result of a catapult strop becoming detached during a launch, 20 June 1951. The pilot, Sub-Lieutenant J. R. Haward, was, happily, rescued.

Main image: The author landing his Fury, VX636 of 801 Squadron, at Hal Far, in July or August of 1952.

passed me, although that thought did not last more than a fraction of a second as I was running out of breath. Inflating my Mae West, I then swam up and at an angle away from where I thought the ship was. I surfaced about twenty to thirty feet away from the ship's side, abeam the starboard propeller, and took a huge breath only to end up choking badly. My oxygen mask was still strapped to my face and the tube attached to the mask was still under the surface. After taking the mask off and getting my breath, I climbed into my dinghy and waited for the lifeboat from the attendant destroyer *Chieftain* to rescue me and then return me to *Glory*.

On reflection, I think that most occasions of RATOG failures on board ships were brought about by the pilot failing to make the master switch. I cannot remember if I made the master switch or not, but I believed that I had. Nevertheless, it was certainly my fault that I went over the bows instead of stopping on the flight deck. Next time I tried, the whole system (including the pilot) worked perfectly.

Once it was established that the Squadron could operate from the deck safely, the emphasis of the flying programme changed. Weapons training now took priority, with divisions of four aircraft operating together strafing, rocketing and bombing (using 11.5-pound practice bombs) against the ship's towed target. Dive bombing with 500-pound bombs took place at Filfla Range just off Malta, while tactical and photographic reconnaissance took place at low level over the desert in Libya. While operating at low level with my division my Number Three, Lieutenant Fiddian-Green, had an engine failure and managed to carry out a wheels-up landing alongside a road near Gnem Fort, south-west of Tripoli. Climbing and reporting his location to the ship, we started the rescue that saw 'Fido' back on board that evening.

During October, the area of operations in which we were able to take part smoothly changed on our way to the Far East. There were navigation exercises in the Red Sea, an exercise strike on Aden and tactical reconnaissance in the Trincomalee area, and at the end of the month we were taking part in anti-bandit sorties in the Kuala Langat area in Malaya. As we carried out these operations over Malaya, *Glory* had to head into wind for the launch and recovery of her aircraft close to two troopships which were on the same heading but en route home. Every two hours *Glory* would reappear at full speed and launch and recover her aircraft and then would disappear.

Below: HMS Glory in Far Eastern waters on 30 January 1952, shortly before she began her second tour of operations against the North Koreans. Nine 812 Squadron Fireflies are ranged aft, four to port and five to starboard, and the remaining aircraft are 804 Squadron's Sea Furies. The slightly different positioning of the wing stripes of the latter is of note: compare those of the four aircraft furthest forward with the remainder. No formal pattern for these stripes was authorised, and each squadron exercised its artistic taste when they were applied. The forward lift (lowered) and the single catapult of these light fleet carriers is clearly evident, as is the outline of the after lift, while the 'batting' platform and its associated safety net can just be seen beneath the port wing tip of the Fury furthest aft on the port side. The two safety barriers (lowered) can be made out amidships, but the arrester wires appear not to have been rigged.

Above: An inquisitive stork makes a vain attempt to carry out a pre-flight cockpit inspection on a chocked and bombed-up Fury. The aircraft's side number is '108', but the full serial number and squadron is unconfirmed.

Above: Another aerial view of *Glory*, taken on the same sortie as was the previous photograph. The *Colossus* class light fleet carriers, an emergency construction programme begun during World War II and utilising merchant-ship scantlings, were, at 16,000 tons, moderate in size, and steady (25 knots) rather than fast in terms of their top speed—but they were absolutely crucial to the prosecution of the Fleet Air Arm's offensive operations during the late 1940s and early 1950s.

We swore that the troopships heeled at least ten degrees towards the carrier every time we went by.

This was a very useful day as it proved to our satisfaction, and to the ship's, that we were capable of meeting one hundred per cent of a day's programme of fully armed bombing sorties. Our journey continued until we paused for three days at Singapore, and we then sailed on to Hong Kong, where we were involved in exercises testing the naval and air defence capabilities of the colony. When the exercises had been completed, *Glory* rendezvoused with her sister *Ocean*, now on her way home from Korea. The two carriers exercised together, and after *Ocean* had transferred five Sea Furies, three Fireflies and two Dragonfly SAR helicopters, and their crews, to *Glory*, the carriers entered Hong Kong harbour together. Two days of briefing then followed involving the Air Department, the Operations Departments, the Carrier Borne Army Liaison Officers (CBALs), the Squadrons, the Air Engineer Officers, the Flight Deck Officers and everyone else caught up in the change from peacetime operations to war. During one briefing by *Ocean*'s CBAL, we heard that we aircrew could forget all we had learned about Escape and Evasion back in Britain. As far as he was aware there was really only one pilot who might get away with it and his name was 'Spiv' Leahy. When challenged, he admitted that it was a friend of mine, 'Hoagy' Carmichael, who had put him up to it. 'Hoagy' was the leader of the division of four Sea Furies from *Ocean* that shot down a MiG-15 (and as far as looks were concerned, he would not have won any beauty competitions either).

On 6 November, leaving *Ocean* to enjoy Hong Kong before continuing on her way home, HMS *Glory* set course for Sasebo in Japan. That evening, *Glory*'s captain was able to report to the Flag Officer of the Far East Station (FO2 FES) that '801 Sea Fury Squadron and 821 Firefly Squadron are now fully worked up and the ship is ready to start her third tour of duty with the United Nations Forces.'

The pattern of operations in which *Glory* was now going take part in consisted of ten days on patrol and ten days off. When on patrol there would be four days of flying operations, one day's replenishment from the Royal Fleet Auxiliary and another four days' flying operations. The ship would then return to Japan, either to Sasebo or to Kure. While the carrier was off station, her place was taken by the USS *Badoeng Strait* or the USS *Bon Homme Richard*, which had Corsairs and Skyraiders embarked. It was originally intended that during the first three days the squadrons would carry out as much area reconnaissance as possible, but the weather was appalling and little was achieved. Most of the aircrew had not had the experience of being shot at, nor were they sure just where they were, flying over seriously inhospitable countryside trying to find a target. The first target for my division of four Sea Furies was in the Sinwon area, north, up the railway from Haeju. When we got there, nothing that looked like a target requiring eight 500-pound bombs was to be seen. I cannot remember what we did with the bombs, but we could not land back on board with them and my log book records 'No joy'.

We immediately settled to our task, which over the weeks ahead took various forms. Interdiction covered operations designed to deprive the enemy of

Above, left and below: The story of a 'prang'. VR938 of 804 Squadron, was touching down on board HMS *Glory* one day in the summer of 1951 when its starboard undercarriage leg gave way—whether or not as a result of a particularly heavy landing is not known. The aircraft took the wire and was brought to a halt, but nevertheless had entwined itself with the barrier and had to be swiftly recovered. It was later lifted off the carrier and on to a barge, transferred to the holding unit at RNAS Sembawang, Singapore, repaired and subsequently returned to Britain.

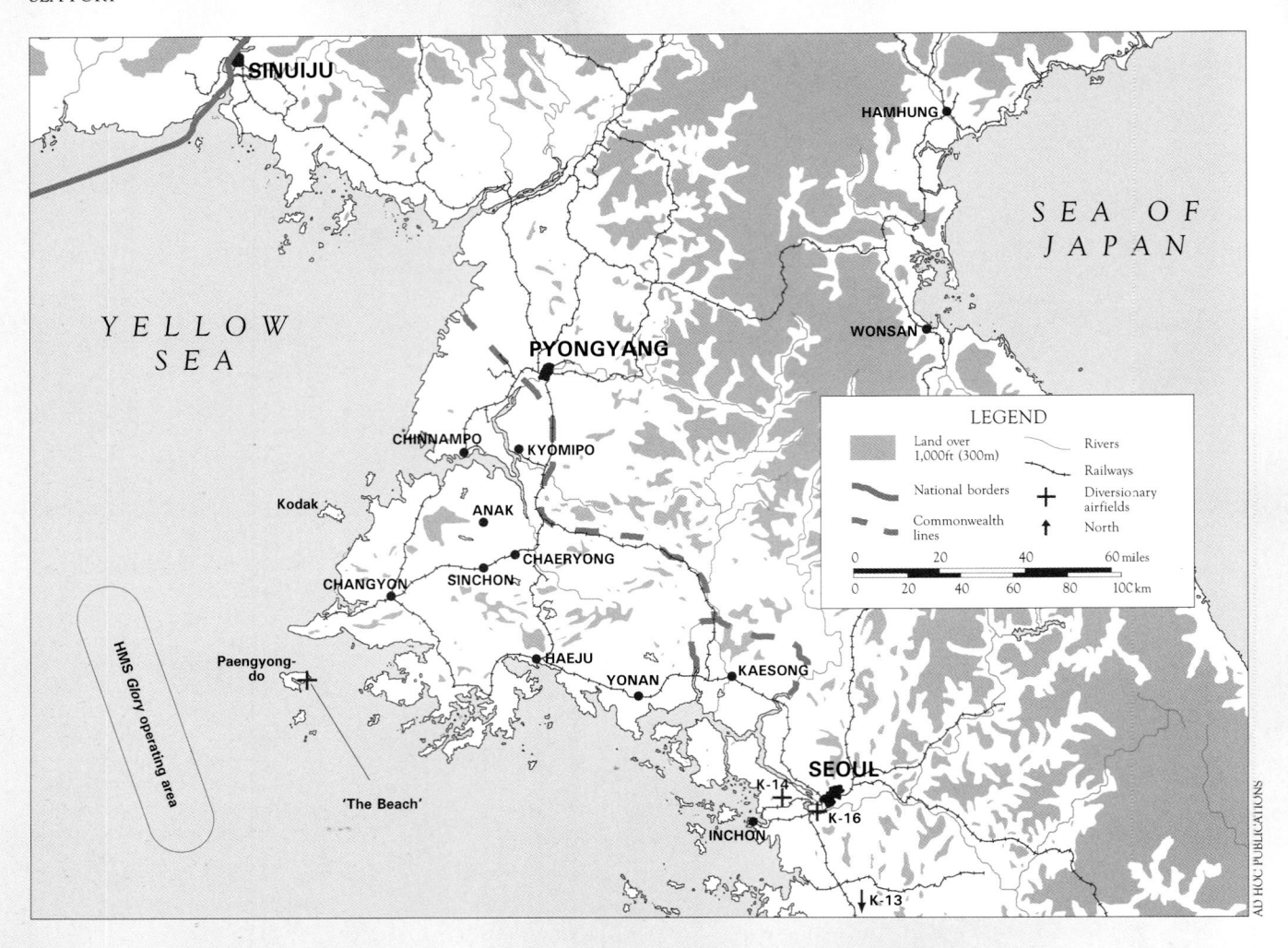

Above: A simplified map showing the area of operations for HMS *Glory* and her squadrons during the winter of 1952/53.

the use of his road and rail communications systems. Road and rail bridges featured often in our list of targets. We used instantaneous-fused 500-pound bombs delivered from a 45-degree dive, and the rule was that the whole division would attack with two-second intervals between aircraft. Once the ordnance had been delivered we would not wait to see what success we had achieved but instead flew off looking for a target for our 20mm cannon, but after twenty or thirty minutes we would return to the original target and fly by at a safe height to check the results.

The trouble with bombing a bridge was that we could come back one or two days later only to find another one in its place. Bombing the railway line some distance away from the bridge was a much more satisfactory operation and could give the North Koreans some aggravation when they tried to move material to fill the holes. Railway tunnels were also attacked, at low level and using bombs with long-delay (30-second) fuses. On one occasion a fuse went off after about fifteen seconds just as my Number Three was about to make his attack. We were informed that the ordnance must have been old World War II stock. We had been briefed that ox carts and men with 'A' frames on their backs were legitimate targets on the basis that ammunition would be moved to the front line by these methods. My division did attack ox carts but they very soon disappeared from the roads, while we never did see a man with an 'A frame. Lorries were considered to be fair game, especially at night. From time to time, once we had become confident of finding our way around our area, we would be launched about an hour and a half before dawn on an armed recce. Pairs would form up and fly off into the area. We had no means of illuminating our targets, but the North Koreans did that for us by driving in large convoys, all the vehicles with their headlights on. Once we had started firing the headlights rapidly went out and we had to pull up as we could no longer see the target or the ground in mountainous terrain. Pilots also lost their wingmen, who now had to set off and look for their own targets. On one occasion I found and attacked five convoys, but it was quite impossible to assess how successful each attack had been.

From time to time we were briefed to attack specific targets. The ship would receive information from partisan forces, which would normally mean that a particular village was occupied by troops. 'Troops in village', in fact, featured quite often as targets and did make us wonder if they were the only occupants, although we had been informed that most of the civilians had been cleared from the coastal areas. Sometimes the ship received information about the success of a particular attack reporting the killed in action (KIA) of any attack. We had no information as to how the partisans were able to move about and gain their information, but Lieutenant Mather, who was shot down, taken prisoner and then marched north to captivity, told me, after his release, that as he was taken north he saw villages stuffed with military equipment and troops.

Pilots, when attacking a village, had to be careful to pick a particular aiming point. If the bombs were dropped with the sight pointed roughly in the middle of the village, with the angle of dive about 45 degrees and the height of release just about correct, the bombs fell around and about and would miss the village—not what was required. There was little point, however, in risking one's life attacking what could be a well-defended target with little hope of success. On one occasion, with Sub-Lieutenant Hayes as my wingman, on only his third sortie, we were attacking a target near Chinnampo and his aircraft was hit by flak. An oil leak was apparent, the engine seized and he had to ditch in amongst small ice floes. Fortunately the Search and Rescue organisation on the island of Chodo, having been alerted, was able to pick him up from the water by SAR helicopter almost immediately. He was transferred to HMAS *Anzac*, on patrol in the vicinity, and returned to *Glory* two days later.

Tactical Air Reconnaissance and Combat Air Patrol (TARCAP) sounds pretty wide-ranging, but it was mainly applied to the task of trying to make life better for the Americans occupying Chodo. Apart from the SAR helicopter, there was a powerful air defence radar which was used to warn of aircraft coming south from China. Their call-sign was 'Mongoose' and they were always quick to offer our aircraft assistance. Across the water on the mainland opposite there were caves in the cliff faces, inside which were guns which would roll out and shell Chodo. The problem was that attacks on their guns appeared to have more success when the latter were firing on Chodo, but their appearance was sporadic. We always had a secondary target which we would use if the North Koreans did not materialise when we were on TARCAP. On one occasion, having dropped our bombs, we searched the road north of

Below: An 801 Squadron Sea Fury engaged in an attack on a target in South Korea; it is on the point of releasing its two 500-pound bombs. What appear to be smaller explosions are occurring close to the main detonation.

AUTHOR'S COLLECTION

Left: Three of 801 Squadron's Sea Furies (circled), photographed by the fourth member of the division at the top of his dive, while attacking a particularly tempting target—the confluence of a rail, road and river system near Chaeryong. The railway line just over the bridge has been hit, as can be seen by the plume of smoke and debris hiding the crossing just over the bridge. Right: This photograph was taken further down in the fourth aircraft's dive and shows two bombs exploding in the water either side of the bridge; at the same time the smoke and debris from the first two aircraft's bombs are drifting away and the crossing has been revealed.

Chinnampo for targets. We attacked three trucks but then found that we had gone too far north and were in the middle of an anti-aircraft barrage on the outskirts of Pyongyang. As we ran south we were told by 'Mongoose' that aircraft had been launched from China and were heading our way. They caught up with us just before we could reach the coast. My Number Three, Lieutenant Fiddian-Green, called a 'break' turn to port to avoid two MiGs, and as I turned I saw that I had a jet, very close behind, firing his 30mm cannon directly at me. By this time we were flying at ninety degrees to his heading and as he had no deflection to allow for our crossing speed we were quickly able to resume our original course, but by this time both the MiGs had passed us and were climbing away, too far out of range.

During air operations there was always a combat air patrol of two Sea Furies. This could be boring—but things could change suddenly. Whenever there was a downed aircraft the CAP would be sent to the area to assist the remaining members of the division protecting or searching for the downed aircrew. Throughout the war several aircrew were saved from capture while waiting for the rescue helicopter to pick them up. On one occasion Lieutenant 'Pug' Mather, who had already been shot down once and rescued by an American helicopter, had to bale out. While the remainder of the division tried to locate 'Pug', the CAP, Sub-Lieutenants Rayner and Keates, were tasked with escorting the SAR helicopter from Chodo. The weather, which had started off bad, was getting steadily worse. The area that was being searched was near Chaeryong, about fifty miles from Chodo, and was very mountainous. The search was eventually called off after Keates lost radio contact with Rayner and then found a large fire on the hillside. Flying was suspended until the afternoon, when aircraft were sent back to the area to continue the search. During this phase of the search, Sub-Lieutenant Simmonds' aircraft was seen to spin in without the pilot being observed attempting to bale out. Our first day back on patrol had not been a successful one.

On a lighter note, when my wingman and I were on CAP we were suddenly vectored north-east towards a threat consisting of a large number of 'bandits' heading towards the ship. As we turned towards the threat, climbing hard, we wondered what we, in our two little Sea Furies, were going to do when we met up with a massed raid of MiG-15s. We were well up towards China, straining to see the MiGs, before we were recalled to our CAP station.

During the debriefing we were told that when we were turned towards the threat the ship had gone to Air Raid Warning Red and was preparing to defend herself. They eventually worked out, however, that they were experiencing a 'mirror radar reflection' (don't ask) of a fighter sweep of F-86 Sabres on their way up to China.

A different sort of task was bombardment spotting, in which we were used to spot for ships firing against the guns opposite Chodo. When the Squadron spotted for the cruiser HMS *Birmingham* we experienced no problems whatever with the communications, the directions to alter their aim or indeed anything at all. However, we were also tasked to bomb-spot for the battleship USS *Missouri* when she came round to the west coast. The first to find himself dealing with the 'Mighty Mo' was our Senior Pilot, Lieutenant Pearce. Having established communications, Pearce was ready to start the drill: 'Standby' ('We are nearly ready'); some time later, 'Shot' ('We have just fired the first sighting shell'); 'Splash' ('The first shell has hit the target'). From his lofty perch, where he could see the target, there was no sign of the fall of shot. Calling for another 'Shot', he waited for the next shell to be fired. Nothing appeared at the call 'Splash', but miles away he saw the result of a shell exploding. In response to his instruction to 'Come left nine miles', things went

Above: In most squadrons, and for the most part, Sea Fury pilots would fly their 'own' aircraft, unless prevented from doing so by the latter's unavailability owing to, for example, the maintenance cycle. The recording of personal names alongside the cockpits was common practice, though that of the number of sorties flown or bombs dropped was less so. These two photographs show detail of the personal aircraft of pilots Lieutenant D. T. McKeown (802 Squadron, HMS *Ocean*) and squadron colleague Lieutenant P. S. Davis, showing their names and those of their maintenance crews, and 'score-boards' relating to the strikes they carried out. Lieutenant McKeown's Fury also displays the Squadron crest, while Lieutenant Davis's markings features a red star, recording his encounter with a MiG that resulted in the latter trailing smoke before disappearing.

Left: A Sea Fury attack on a small village, carried out in response to a request by partisans.

Opposite page: A Sea Fury (circled) pulls out of an attack. Vortices, indicating high 'g' forces, can just be made out streaming from the wing tips.

very quiet and he lost all communication with the ship! Lieutenant-Commander Robert McCandless recalls similar experiences on page 84 of this book.

I was next on the flying programme when *Glory* was required to provide bomb-spot. I established communication with the 'Mighty Mo' and all went well until the first shell was fired. I was flying with the target clearly visible below, to the south, when there was a sudden *whoosh* and my Sea Fury jumped into the air. Looking round to see what had happened, I was just in time to spy a huge shell, at my height and slowly rotating, disappearing to the east. When I tried to remonstrate with the battleship all communication ceased and that was the end of that bomb-spot.

A further task for our Squadron was close air support (CAS) of the Commonwealth Division. Before we took part in these activities, however, Lieutenant Pearce and I visited the 3rd Royal Australian Regiment on the front line while *Glory* was back in Japan. Our route to the front line was from the ship to K 16, an airfield south of Seoul, courtesy of the USN carrier onboard delivery aircraft. These COD aircraft (TBM-3Cs) delivered personnel and mail to the carrier on patrol, and they and their pilots had a very high reputation for their reliability and safety. Unfortunately one pilot, Lieutenant (jg) Homer, was unlucky enough to be involved in a barrier accident on board *Glory*. He said after the accident that he feared what his CO would do to him for blotting their copy-book reputation! After our arrival at K 16, Lieutenant Pearce and I were then taken by jeep up to the front line, and on the second day we were taken for a tour along the 3rd RAR portion of the front. While we were there an Australian patrol upset the Chinese and we were subjected to a barrage of mortar fire which lasted for more than an hour.

When we were tasked for CAS flights we were required to check in with our bomb load en route. After a short spell holding off we would be allocated to a 'Mosquito' (no relation to de Havilland), a small aircraft based just south of front line, which would indicate our target by firing a rocket to mark the target with smoke. I was not surprised that we could not see the target, marked by the smoke, having survived a barrage on the ground which apparently came out of nowhere, but we would get reports

69

afterwards, for example 'Four caves damaged, one mortar position', 'Five mortar positions destroyed' and 'Three shelters destroyed and one damaged'.

Apart from K 16, where we landed when Pearce and I went to the front, there was also, south of Seoul, K 13, which was fully operational with F-86s, F-84s and B-26s stationed there. Whenever we had a hung bomb—that is, one that did not release—we were able to divert to K 13 as it was not a good idea to try to land back on the ship with a live bomb that you had already tried to shake off. Normally it was possible to have the bomb removed at K 13 and then land back on board at the next recovery. On one occasion my wingman, Lieutenant Peter Wheatley, and I were airborne on the last sortie of a patrol and he had a hung bomb which meant that we had to divert to K 13 while our carrier set off for Japan and left us to sort ourselves out. We were accommodated by a very hospitable F-84 squadron whose aircrew inhabited a large Nissan type of hut. At the far end of the hut was a well-stocked bar, and it was approaching midnight before we remembered that we had not diluted the oil in the engines: as it was a very cold night, −20ºC, we had to get back to the flight line and run up Furies. Next morning we set off back to the line and carried out a full daily inspection of our aircraft as the students had been taught back at Culdrose. When we were ready to go, however, my starter did not fire, so I had to climb out of the cockpit and ask one of the ground crew to get me a hammer. While he went to get one I opened the large panel on top of the cowling just behind the engine. The problem was that the Coffman starter could get jammed with carbon, which stopped the barrel of the starter clicking round and lining up the next cartridge to be fired. All that was normally required to cure this snag was to give the Coffman a sharp blow with a hammer to dislodge the carbon. When the airman returned with the hammer I dealt the Sea Fury a nasty blow. Having seen that the next cartridge had clicked into place I handed back the hammer, thanked the crewman and replaced the cowling. With both Sea Furies running smoothly, we taxied out, leaving behind some rather bemused USAF personnel. When we had climbed up to our cruising height en route to Iwakuni airfield near Kure, where the carrier was heading, we noticed an F-84 turning in as if to attack us. Remembering that all aircraft airborne in the area probably had a full load of ammunition on board, we acted aggressively and turned hard towards him and, possibly remembering the same thing, he turned away and went about his business. While turning towards the F-84 my engine

Below: The author in his aircraft, WJ295 '159/R', preparing to move forward to HMS Glory's catapult for launching on another strike against enemy targets in the Korean peninsula. The aircraft carries two 45-gallon drop tanks and two 500-pound bombs—the standard warload for 801 Squadron's Furies during this phase of the operations. Two flight deck handlers are in position to remove the chocks when signalled to do so.

Above: VR937 of 804 Squadron—on board *Glory* during the carrier's first two tours of duty (801 was on board for the third and last)—bounced while landing on 28 June 1951, missed the wires and ended up in the barrier, which pitched the aircraft on to its nose. The pilot, Commissioned Pilot B. J. Potts, was uninjured. The Sea Fury was later repaired.

started to hesitate when 'g' was applied, but once flying straight and level it smoothed out—until, that is, we were crossing the Korea Strait towards Japan, when the hesitations restarted in 1g flight and became more frequent. Crossing the Japanese coast, I could see Itazuki airfield ahead and so I declared an emergency and asked permission to land, but this was refused as there was a large crane on the runway. Itazuki was a big airfield, used by the US Air Force, and I could see the crane heading towards me on one side of the wide runway. I apologised, telling them I had no alternative, and landed on the other side, passing the crane with room to spare. I received every assistance once I had explained my problem, and it was arranged that I would leave my Sea Fury with them until it could be repaired. My wingman was able to arrange for a Firefly to come and collect me so that I could re-join the carrier at Kure.

We occasionally flew armed reconnaissance sorties: we used to think that if The Powers That Be could not think of anything better to do, they launched us without bombs to see what we could turn up. My wingman and I were attacking a target on one of these sorties when there was a loud explosion. I was very surprised as I had not seen any signs of any ground fire, but when I looked at my port wing I saw that there was a large hole in it and, aft, the port tailplane was waving at me in my mirror. Climbing cautiously and heading for the sea in case I had to ditch or bale out, I called my wingman and asked him to have a look and see what the damage was like at the tail. Closing in, all he had to offer was the opinion that it seemed as though it was going to fall off. How to improve your leader's morale! We were about 40–50 miles away from Paengyong-do, an island just off the coast and occupied by friendly forces. There was a long beach on the island where it was possible to land Sea Furies,

Above: VR943 ('105/R' is bombed up preparatory to a sortie on board HMS *Glory*, spring or early summer 1951, during the carrier's first Korean tour. This is an 804 Squadron aircraft. Notice the vacant rocket rails either side of the bomb carrier.
Right: Two stages in the demise of a mystery Sea Fury, which may have struck the round-down or have experienced a torque stall during an attempt to land-on. The carrier is indisputably HMS *Glory*: her identification letter, 'R', being present on the port quarter of the flight deck. For further details, see the following pages.

Fireflies and Dakotas. 'Wounded' aircraft, like my Sea Fury, were welcome there, as were the Fireflies which flew in to pick up the pilots and take them back to *Glory*. Having gently climbed high enough to enable me to bale out in a hurry if the tailplane decided to give up the ghost, I determined, when I could see Paengyong-do, to find out, even more gently, what the effect would be were I to select wheels and flaps down and settle for an approach speed of 110 knots. Considering the state that the Sea Fury was in, it behaved perfectly and I was able to carry out a landing on the beach, and after landing I was able to taxi to the end of the beach, where I was directed to park. (Did I remember to lock my tail wheel before landing ashore? I have no idea!) When I climbed out of the cockpit I was able to examine the damage and stand with head and shoulders sticking up through the hole in the wing (see photograph on page 80). During this patrol, two days previously, a Firefly was seen to have suffered an explosion in the wing and the aircraft had crashed, killing the pilot. It was later found out that the 20mm ammunition being used was of 1943 vintage, and as a result we were banned from firing our cannon, unless defensively, until better ammunition had been supplied. Some time afterwards Lieutenant Wheatley nursed his Sea Fury back to Paengyong-do with his oil temperature going off the clock and successfully landed, wheels up, on the beach; on an earlier occasion he had carried out a forced landing, with his wheels down, at Hal Far and had seen the bits of engine, including part of a piston ring, that fell to the ground when the engine cowling had later been opened, so he was not prepared to take any chances.

During HMS *Ocean*'s time on station before *Glory* relieved her, she had flown a total of 123 sorties in a day. Our captain, Captain E. D. G. Lewin, and the ship's staff considered that, with 33 aircraft and 50 pilots, it should be possible to launch a total of 200 sorties. Accordingly it was decided to arrange to try to surpass *Ocean*'s record. Easter Sunday, 5 April, was chosen to be the day. Our squadron pilots were scheduled for four sorties each, two of us being allocated five. The first launch took place just before dawn, at 0645. My division's target was the Haeju marshalling yard, and after the attack I reported that we had cut the track at the entrance. Our second launch was at 0925 and this time our target was a

INTO ACTION

SEA FURY

INTO ACTION

This spread: What is odd about this incident is that it does not appear to have been officially recorded—or, at least, that the records relating to it have become mislaid. The first four digits of the aircraft's serial number are V, X, 6, and 3, and the side number is plain to see. The only candidate that seems to fit the bill is VX636, but the archives indicate that this particular aircraft was merely 'struck off charge', from *Glory*, in September 1952 (that is, while the ship was in the Mediterranean). This date also points to the Fury being an 801 Squadron aircraft. It is fairly clear that the aircraft irretrievably disappeared as a result of the incident, and thus the SOC date was probably the date the incident took place, although, interestingly, none of the personnel serving on board the ship at this time who have been contacted can recall it. There is no mention of a pilot's name for VX636, but one secondary source in referring to this sequence of photographs states that the pilot survived the accident and was rescued by the attendant destroyer.

75

SEA FURY

Above: An 804 Squadron Sea Fury departs via HMS *Glory*'s catapult. The standard Royal Navy catapult of the time, the BH 3, was a pneumatic/hydraulic device with a track 140 feet 9 inches long and could carry out up to 1,000 launches of a fully armed Sea Fury before requiring major overhaul—usually attended to in the dockyard although, if necessary, at sea.

Main image: The very significant contribution to the Korean operations by the Royal Australian Navy should never be overlooked, and the light fleet carrier HMAS *Sydney*—formerly HMS *Terrible*, and a near-sister ship of the British carriers of the *Colossus* class—conducted an offensive patrol between September 1951 and January 1952 (between *Glory*'s first and second patrols). Like her Royal Navy counterparts, she flew Sea Furies (805 and 808 Squadrons) and Fireflies (817). Here WE676 of 808 Squadron makes a safe landing.

railway bridge north of Haeju, which we destroyed. The third launch was at 1205 and again our target was a railway bridge; again, we destroyed it. The fourth launch was made at 1445 and the target was, once more, north of Haeju. I cannot remember what that target was, but 'No joy' is recorded in my log book. Finally, as far as I was concerned, the last launch took place at 1705, when my wingman and I were sent up on CAP. The last recovery was at 1925, and 123 sorties had been flown by the air group, equalling *Ocean*'s record.

* * *

HMS *Glory*'s last patrol came to an end when she met up with *Ocean* at Sasebo and handed her duties over to her and her aircraft, 807 (Sea Fury) and 810 (Firefly) Squadrons.

Notwithstanding the fact that in my division of four aircraft there had been four forced landings as a result of engine problems during the time we had been working up in the Mediterranean and then operating in the Far East, the Sea Furies had proved to be, on the whole, remarkably serviceable. When we were on patrol it was necessary to have a deck park at all times. We were subjected to the full spectrum of bad weather—gales, freezing rain, snow, freezing fog and extreme cold. In the midst of all this, the groundcrew had to service the aircraft on deck when the carrier was under 'Darken Ship' conditions. Each aircraft had two 'owners', the pilot and the Pilot's Mate, and the preference was that the pilot would always fly his 'own' aircraft. This, however, was not always possible: for example, if that aircraft was in the hangar and the deck park was full, it just had to stay where it was. I was not popular with the groundcrew when I put my Fury in the Mediterranean, but I think I was forgiven when I had to leave one on the beach at Paengyong-do.

When we arrived in the Far East we had eighteen aircrew; when we left, only ten of the original eighteen remained, although our pilot strength was maintained at eighteen. 'Pug' Mather, we thought, had not survived being shot down twice, but it transpired that he had been taken prisoner and had survived that as well. Another pilot had problems and had to be sent home. Of the other casualties, most had crashed while attacking targets, although one pilot was killed while attempting to ditch alongside the ship. Of those who survived, it is unlikely that any were able to achieve, again, the intensity of carrier flying that was experienced during our time on operations off Korea.

Korean Snowstorm *Lieutenant-Commander Robert McCandless DSC*

After the war I joined 1830 Squadron (the RNVR's Scottish Air Division) while I was attending the Heriot-Watt College in Edinburgh. We flew from RNAS Abbotsinch, which is now Glasgow Airport. At that time, the Squadron had Harvards, Fireflies and Seafires. It was a carefree time and we thoroughly enjoyed our flying. My job then moved me to work in Liverpool, and I continued to fly with 1831 Squadron based at Stretton. There I was introduced to Sea Furies and these were, without doubt as far as I am concerned, the very best aircraft I have ever flown. (I never had the opportunity to fly a Sea Hornet, which I understand, was even better—but one cannot have everything.) This was about the time of the start of the Korean campaign in terms of Fleet Air Arm operations, and when I was told that there was a shortage of aircrew I decided to re-join the Service. I thought I was particularly lucky to be sent to Culdrose to be brought up to date in the Fighter School, flying Sea Furies. After that I was sent to Lee-on-Solent to join 801 Squadron, which was at that time working up for deployment to Korea. We finally joined HMS *Glory*, arriving in the combat area on 11 November 1952.

The ship's operating pattern was to have nine days on patrol with a refuelling and resupply day at sea in the middle, then a spell in either Sasebo or Kure in Japan, where the repair ship HMS *Unicorn* would carry out any repairs or provide replacement aircraft. We alternated with an American carrier, the USS *Baedong Strait*, which was operating Corsairs flown by US Marine Corps pilots.

The weather in that part of the world in winter can be bitterly cold and, as far as we were concerned, very unpredictable. For those working on the flight deck, the conditions were truly miserable, but we nevertheless managed to maintain the air activity required by those in strategic command. This was achieved with the minimum number of accidents, to the extent that the aircrews in the Fireflies and Sea Furies managed over 1,000 deck landings without incident, including pre-dawn take-offs and after-dusk landings. There is no doubt that this gave us a great feeling of satisfaction and confidence.

One of the difficulties in the situation was that all the weather approached us from over China, so there were no weather reports from that quarter, making forecasting very difficult for the Met Officer. There was one occasion when the forecast was particularly 'variable'. We flew off a flight of four Fireflies and my own flight of four Sea Furies, with two Sea Furies for CAP. The two flights of four were given specific targets, alternative targets or army co-operation over the front line. This last was always a tricky business because the US Air Force pilots over the same area on the same frequency seemed to talk continuously on subjects other than target information. If we had not been detailed for army co-operation, we would fly around at about 5,000 feet, looking for targets of opportunity—that is, anything that moved in the area for which we were responsible on the North Korean side of the line.

Part way through the sortie we were recalled to the ship because the weather was deteriorating rapidly. By the time we got back to the ship the two Sea Fury CAP aircraft had landed-on but the ship herself had disappeared into a snowstorm. The Fireflies orbited at 800 feet and I kept my flight at 1,200 feet while we waited to see if any breaks would come along. Twice they did, but did not last long enough for us to get down. By now, the shore diversion was also snow-bound. A third break came along after an apprehensive wait and the Fireflies dived down into the circuit with the four of us in our Sea Furies in hot pursuit. The gap was just long enough, luckily, otherwise there could have been a disaster for the ship and a very nasty outcome for the twelve aircrew.

Left and opposite, top: The Korean winters could be harsh—harsh enough occasionally to curtail flying. Even so, the daily routine of aircraft maintenance and preparation had to continue, often on deck, where personnel were exposed to the full force of snowstorms and freezing temperatures. Fireflies tended to be more susceptible to the conditions than the Sea Furies, the former's inline Griffon engines sometimes experiencing leaks as their metal pipework contracted with the cold. These two photographs offer a glimpse of the difficulties caused by the severe weather.

Opposite, centre: Ice floes were another sort of problem in the winter, at least for Allied ships working close inshore. Here two Sea Furies of 801 Squadron carry out a TARCAP (Tactical Air Reconnaissance and Combat Air Patrol).

Tale of a Trim Tab *Commander Robin Foster* OBE

In February 1951 a Sea Fury flown from HMS *Theseus* had to land at Suwon, thirty miles south of Seoul, with half a propeller blade missing; there was also a Firefly which needed a new mainplane. I was flown with AA3 O'Brien and four junior ratings to Suwon in a US Air Force C-119 Flying Boxcar with a spare propeller and the replacement mainplane projecting out of the rear.

At Suwon, there were four inches of snow and we were dressed in normal uniform and raincoats—totally unsuitable wear for a Korean winter. The Army rose to the occasion, however, providing us with food and a tent, together with much-needed winter combat clothing.

Next day I left O'Brien and the team to get on with the repairs and went to USAF Base Ops to try and arrange for a crane to hold the propeller for the change. The first question I was asked was, 'Where are your orders?' Of course, I had nothing in writing—just a verbal directive:

'There is a problem. Go and fix it!' It did not help that I was dressed in an Army Parka jacket with no badges or anything to show that I was a Naval officer. I eventually left with a possible promise of a crane sometime the next afternoon. Chastened, I went back to the aircraft to discover that a USAF sergeant had called, and the gist of the conversation was that he had a crane and understood that we had access to some grog. Next morning a bottle of whisky changed hands and we had the full use of a crane for both jobs for the whole day.

While the work was going on, the USAF sent any aircraft from *Theseus*, either with minor defects or just to get mail, to our part of the airfield, for refuelling, etc. On completion of the two jobs we returned to Japan.

As a result of this experience it was agreed that we should have a permanent presence ashore in Korea, comprising a CPO and a couple of junior rates, to be supplemented from the Aircraft Holding Unit in Japan as necessary. Initially they were at Suwon, then, as the front line moved north, they moved to Kimpo, and finally they were relocated to the British air head at Yongdongpo just outside Seoul. This proved a great success.

Off the south-west corner of the North Korean peninsula are a number of islands, the south-westernmost of which is Paengyong-do. It has a long, hard, sandy beach which at half-tide down makes a very good airstrip. This was regularly used by the USAF and occasionally as an emergency landing strip by the Royal Navy. On four occasions we flew over in a Dakota to sort out problems that would have rendered deck landing inadvisable, for example, flak damage, a stuck-up arrester hook, or a rough-running engine. In September 1951 a combined operation was mounted with the maintenance carrier *Unicorn* and the frigate *St Brides Bay*, a US Navy landing craft and a US Army 15-ton crane to collect a Firefly and a Sea Fury from

Opposite, top: A wintry scene on board HMS *Theseus*, 1950/51.
Opposite, bottom: Sea Fury WJ295 on 'The Beach' at Paengyong-do, December 1952. This is author Alan Leahy's aircraft; the events leading up to the emergency landing are described on pages 71–72.
Right: 'Wounded' aircraft that could not be repaired on board the parent carrier were transferred to the maintenance carrier HMS *Unicorn*, generally stationed out of harm's way in Japanese waters. Here an 804 Squadron Sea Fury (lacking underwing serials) and an unidentified Firefly are being moved to the ship by lighter.
Below: HMS *Unicorn*. During the Korean War she acted not only as a heavy repair ship but also as a training carrier.

Paengyong-do. Five of us embarked in the LCU, with the crane, at Inchon and were escorted to Paengyong-do by *St Brides Bay*, and we secured alongside her at anchor in the lee of the island. Next day we beached and unloaded the crane. The Fury had landed at almost high water, so there was little available hard sand; the starboard oleo had encountered the soft stuff above the high-water mark and been wrenched off.

The crane lifted the aircraft and we fitted a jury leg, lowered away and then, with the crane acting as a tractor, started to move the aircraft from the soft sand to the hard. The jury leg objected to this and completely buckled. Luckily my original brief had been slightly confused, and I was uncertain as to whether both oleos had collapsed or only one, so we had taken two jury legs with us. The second was fitted, and now, with the crane taking a lot of the weight of the aircraft as well as acting as the tractor, we very gingerly moved from the soft stuff to the hard sand. Once we were on the beach proper no problems were encountered, and the Fury was loaded into the LCU. The Firefly was then brought to the LCU, but we discovered that we could not get both aircraft on board as the Fury's tailplane was four inches too wide to fit between the LCU's after superstructure. The solution was to remove the tailplane—simple for the most part, but the trim tab control wire was right inside and almost out of sight with a very small nut and bolt to secure the two ends together. After struggling for over thirty minutes to undo the connection, and very conscious that we still had to load the Firefly, the tide was inexorably rising and we had *Unicorn* waiting to sail, I cut the wire. We then loaded the aircraft, unbeached, offloaded to *Unicorn* and returned to Inchon. Months later I was reprimanded by Sembawang as it took them over three days to re-thread a new trim tab wire!

SEA FURY

Friendly Fire *Lieutenant-Commander Tom Leece*

I checked out on the Sea Fury in May 1949 and flew it for 948 hours. During that time I clocked up 299 deck landings with one tenth-wire barrier! I also flew the Mk 20 two-seat trainer version during a spell with 1832 Squadron RNVR at RAF Benson. Without doubt the Sea Fury was an excellent all-round naval day fighter-bomber and a very good deck-lander in the days of the axial-deck aircraft carriers—an opinion that was shared by every Fury pilot I knew. Another big 'plus' was its ability to remain airborne for a long time, with sorties of up to three hours being planned and flown during the Korean War. In the early days there was some doubt about the reliability of the Centaurus engine, which had caused a number of forced landings. I had two of them, but the problems were overcome and the engine was generally liked and described as being really smooth.

The first of my forced landings occurred in August 1952 while we were operating in the Eastern Med from *Glory*. We had been briefed for a high-altitude sortie, but the engine stopped and I landed wheels-up on an overgrown disused airstrip in Cyprus. Luckily I missed hitting an old Turkish farmer who was working there, and as I climbed out of the cockpit he came over and gave me a nice big watermelon to eat while I waited for the rescue squad to get me out! The second forced landing was in February 1953. Four Sea Furies had to be ferried from Britain to Malta and the Navy decided to use the opportunity to break the speed record. Lieutenant 'Gus' Halliday and I were briefed to lead a section on separate flights. My section took off from Lee-on-Solent and climbed to 20,000-plus feet, and we were over the snow-capped Alps with various summits poking through extensive cloud cover when my engine stopped. I thought about baling out, but my hands were almost frozen (there was no heating in those days) and so I decided to remain on course and glide across southern France to the Med and then ditch. I had my wingman with me and he looked after radio communication whilst I sorted out my landing problem. Our track took us over Nice, and as we approached the coast the cloud cover broke and I saw a large aerodrome to port. I was able to position for a wheels-down landing (landing downwind) and turn off the runway before coming to a dead stop. A fire truck came up quickly and I learned that I was at Nice Airport and that a BEA Viking had to delay its take-off for London on account of my unexpected arrival. However, the French were very understanding and the British Consul eventually arrived and took good care of us. He checked us in to a very good hotel and advised us to take taxis as needed. 'And by the way,' he said, 'it is Battle of the Flowers Week. I hope you have a good time.' And we did! The problem had been caused by the engine supercharger blades breaking up. Gus and his wingman, incidentally, did make it to Malta, and they did break the record.

An episode during the Korean War vouches for the toughness of the Fury. Whilst flying Number Two to Charlie Lavender, I noticed, and reported to Charlie, that two US Corsair aircraft were operating below us. We watched them attack a target and then turn towards us; we thought they were about to join us to say hello. All our Navy aircraft had been painted with large black and white stripes on the upper and lower surfaces of each wing (similar to the markings used during the D-Day operations of World War II), and it therefore came as a nasty surprise when the Corsairs opened fire on my aircraft. They were very close behind and I noticed tracer bullets hitting each wing. I rapidly broke starboard and could see that the upper surface of the starboard wing was glowing bright red and that smoke was pouring out behind me. The controls felt heavy and I knew that we were badly damaged. However, the engine had not been hit and within a short time the glow in the wing died away and we were still flying. We were some miles over north-eastern Korea and the two

Corsairs were now attacking Charlie so I headed back to our ship, HMS *Theseus*, checked the flap operation etc. and the stalling speed and landed-on safely. There were about thirty bullet holes in both wings. The trim controls had been shot away, and the fire had gone out because the lower wing surface had been burnt through and the remaining fuel had dropped out. In talking about it afterwards we figured that the only reason the engine and pilot were not hit was that the Americans were too close behind when they opened fire and their gun harmonisation was concentrating their firepower some distance ahead of my aircraft. Lucky me!

One last story. A small group of pilots had been flown out to Hong Kong to join the first Sea Fury squadron to operate in Korea, 807 on board *Theseus*. We had not flown for some days and we joined a few RAF personnel who were stationed at Kai Tak aerodrome. We had to practise general flying but concentrate on ADDLs. It was during one of these sorties that our temporary leader, Lieutenant Charles Debney, taxied out to take off, spread his folded wings and lined up on the runway. The Kai Tak runway was rather short and ended abruptly at the Hong Kong harbour, which was used by the RAF as a flying-boat base. Charles (as he was always known) had opened the throttle and was accelerating towards the sea when, to his consternation, he saw his starboard wing folding up. He tried his best to stop but the Fury reached the end of the runway and toppled into the harbour. Charles sat in the cockpit up to his chest in water. The RAF later sent him a Christmas card bearing a photograph of the Sea Fury bravely saluting as it plunged into the sea!

Below: Sea Furies of 807 Squadron and Fireflies of 810 Squadron jostle for space forward on HMS *Theseus*'s flight deck. This carrier undertook one tour of duty in Korean waters, lasting from September 1950 until April 1951. The aircraft are in smart condition; some have only a partial suite of black and white stripes and a couple have none at all.

International Co-operation *Lieutenant-Commander Robert McCandless* DSC

One of the more unusual tasks I was given to carry out during my time in HMS *Glory* off Korea was to spot during a bombardment by the USS *Missouri* (the 'Mighty Mo'). My Number Two and I headed for the rendezvous off the west coast of Korea, north of the 38th Parallel, where there was a battery of fairly heavy artillery hidden away from bombing attacks in caves in a high cliff-face. These guns were harassing UN ships operating along that coast and the Americans had decided to stop the harassment.

The 'Mighty Mo' was a magnificent ship and I was very impressed when we first sighted her. We established good, clear communication, confirmed the position of the target, and went off to take up our position some ten or more miles away to see clearly the fall of shot.

The ship called 'Ready', so I made sure I was in a good position and not in the line of fire and replied, 'Ready.'

MM: 'Shot—thirteen seconds.'
Self: (After a long pause) 'Not observed.'
MM: 'Ready.'
Self: 'Ready.'
MM: 'Shot—thirteen seconds.'
Self: (After another very long pause) 'Not observed.'

By this time I was becoming very concerned. This was my first operational attempt at spotting for a bombardment, and I was wondering what I was doing that was so wrong.

MM: 'Ready.'

Even in that one word I could hear their frustration, and I could imagine someone muttering, 'Open your bloody eyes!' So, before I responded, I decided to watch more carefully inland because there had been no splashes in the sea from the first two shots

Self: 'Ready.'
MM: 'Shot—thirteen seconds.'

This time I did see where the shell exploded—and it was a long way inland.

Self: 'Observed—approximately two miles over.'
MM: (Most unbelieving) 'Are you sure?'
Self: 'Wait—I'll pass a six-figure map reference.'
Self: 'Map reference of the fall of shot is ——.'
MM: 'Roger. Wait.'
MM: (After another very long wait) 'Ready.'
Self: 'Ready.'
MM: 'Shot—thirteen seconds.'

The fall of shot was right at the base of the cliff.

Self: 'Target. Fire for effect.'
MM: 'Ready.'
Self: 'Ready.'
MM: 'Shot—thirteen seconds.'

And was it ever effective! Nine sixteen-inch shells demolished the entire cliff face for over a hundred yards and it all fell into the sea.

Self: 'Target. Very effective. No sign of any remaining caves or armament.'
MM: 'Roger. Thank you. Out.'

At the end of that particular nine-day patrol, we returned to Kure for R&R and replacement aircraft as well as normal replenishment. Lo and behold—there was the 'Mighty Mo', also in harbour. At lunchtime I was given a message: an American officer wished to speak to me. When I went up on to the quarterdeck, there stood a USN Commander. I confirmed that I was the pilot of the spotting aircraft and he then apologised profusely for the confusion during the bombardment—there had been a malfunction in the plotting table. A very good lunch was had by all.

Everybody's Favourite *Vice-Admiral Sir Edward Anson* KCB FRAeS

As for many Fleet Air Arm pilots of my generation, my flying got under way with Percival Prentices at RAF Syerston, then moving on to Harvards. The next stage in my training involved a transfer to RNAS Lossiemouth to begin flying Seafires, and from these I moved on to the more powerful Sea Fury, the radial Centaurus of which made for a much wider nose and a rather more difficult view forward for the pilot.

Part of our combat training was undertaken at RNAS Treligga, a bombing and gunnery range near RNAS St Merryn. Here we practised dummy dives in our Furies using the gun camera fitted in the wing leading edge. Concentric circles had been marked out at the range, but of course at the 45-degree angle at which we were diving these took on the appearance of concentric ellipses. We were instructed to press the bomb release button once when the dive was first entered, and press it a second time at the point when the bomb would have been released. Once we had landed back at St Merryn (Treligga had no runway), the Wrens would remove the film and process it, and the frames would be displayed on a screen that was tilted backwards at 45 degrees, thereby converting the ellipses back into circles and enabling the accuracy of each pilot's 'bombing' to be assessed.

Deck-landing training was of course another essential part of our conversion into proficient Naval pilots, initially taking the form of Aerodrome Dummy Deck Landings (ADDLs) in co-operation with 767 Squadron at RNAS Yeovilton and, later, RNAS Henstridge before we made our first practice landings on board the training carrier. The Sea Fury took a bit of getting used to, and there were two occasions when I went into the barrier. We had been trained that, in the event of missing the wire, we should try to point the aircraft at the centre of the barrier as this would minimise the damage to the aircraft. Fortunately, on both occasions I managed to find the centre. There were always techniques to be followed—even in the event of an accident!

It was not long before we saw action. In December 1952 I joined 801 Squadron on board HMS *Glory*. The Korean War had been raging for two and a half years. My service in

Above: Sea Fury Mk 11 WJ266 of 801 Squadron on board HMS *Glory* and carrying, inboard, two 45-gallon fuel tanks, that beneath the starboard wing having been locally modified to accept a camera installation—a 'store' commonly carried on strike sorties for evaluating the success or otherwise of an attack. What appear to be bombs on the outboard pylons are in fact canisters containing leaflets; these were dropped in a dive and set to open at altitude for good distribution. Notice that the aircraft's call-sign ('side number') is repeated beneath the engine cowling and, in abbreviated form, on the main undercarriage doors. Very unusually, this aircraft has its underwing serials painted white rather than black; the reason for this is unknown.

Far Eastern waters was to last until June 1953, on completion of 98 sorties (during which time, in May 1953, I had transferred to 807 Squadron on board *Glory*'s sistership HMS *Ocean*). Now all our hard training was put to the test. Speed, accuracy and efficiency were the order of the day, and the learning process bonding man and machine continued to develop. Our deck-landing skills became ever more proficient, and we also learned to take account of the aircraft's little nuances that would be of benefit in the approach and touch-down. For example, turning from the downwind leg with 2,400 revs, the Fury would gradually settle down into the approach so that when it crossed the round-down everything was just right. However, much still depended upon the batsman. We had one called 'Tiny' Bowen, and he was excellent because he just tended to hold a 'Roger' and let the pilot get on with the job of landing his aircraft; in contrast another, who shall be nameless, behaved as if he himself was flying the aircraft, not coaxing another pilot down safely, and indulged in such exaggerated gestures that on one occasion the carrier received a signal from the attendant destroyer commenting on his overly balletic tendencies. I quickly learned to ignore him!

Our principal task was bombing; these days one would call it ground attack or close air support. We would attack from about 4,000 feet and let go with both bombs in a 45-degree dive (as practised at Treligga). The standard procedure was to release both together; dropping one and then returning for a second pass was hazardous in the extreme, since the enemy gunners were alert and would no doubt have found the range the second time round. Even so, there were some (again, nameless!) who favoured two passes at a target. Possibly they were trying to prove something, but in reality it was a foolhardy tactic. I was hit once by anti-aircraft fire, down in the tail, where the airframe skinning was thin. I was sitting in the wardroom after we had returned, when one of the fitters asked whether I would like to take a look at my aeroplane. I went down into the hangar, and, taking a broomstick, he demonstrated. 'You was hit here, sir,' he explained, indicating by pushing the broomstick through the gap, 'and it came out here,' as the stick emerged from the other side of the fuselage, The 40mm shell had passed right through the aircraft, providentially missing all the control wires within. 'You was very lucky, sir.' I was indeed.

As well as undertaking bombing sorties, all Fury pilots had to carry out combat air patrol over the ship as a part of their duties, These did not 'count' in the tally of sorties undertaken, although on one occasion, while I was preparing to undertake a CAP with the CO (the weather was so bad that no other flying was possible), I instead found myself flying towards land as at the last moment we received a signal from Korean partisans requesting that we strike an island that they had identified. The call was urgent, and so the brief was hastily revised and off we went. The Furies' 20mm guns did the job.

The Sea Fury was an excellent aeroplane, and once its little foibles had been mastered it was everybody's favourite. It is very fondly remembered.

FRONT-LINE SEA FURY SQUADRONS

The Sea Fury is but one name on the lengthy list of British military aircraft that were conceived during World War II but were unable to take part in combat operations because hostilities drew to a close before they could reach the squadrons. However, unlike other advanced designs that reached prototype stage, the Fury was held to be of such significance that, in its naval incarnation, it was allowed to proceed to the status of quantity production after the war. Moreover, in receiving approval as a carrier-based fighter, it was not, unlike many of its land-based fighter contemporaries, cancelled merely because it was not a jet aircraft: although a jet-powered Vampire had successfully landed on board a ship under way in 1945, it was quickly apparent that much more work was required to ensure that everyday on-board arrivals by such aircraft could be conducted safely and efficiently. In 1945, the end of the era of the piston-engined fighter was, for the Navy, by no means in sight.

With many of the basic proving trials out of the way by the time the war ended, and the production lines for the Fury already busy, it was not long before the first Mk Xs were released for service trials. 778 Naval Air Squadron at Ford took delivery of its first aircraft in the spring of 1947, and by the end of the summer of that year 803 and 807 Squadrons had received their new equipment. 802 and 805, the latter a Royal Australian Navy unit, had been issued with Furies by the summer of 1948, by which time production of the Mk X had ceased, its place on the line having been taken by the more capable F. B. Mk XI. Indeed, 803 and 807 had already begun to re-equip with the new variant in February 1948, and by the end of the year 802 and 805 were beginning to exchange their Furies also.

The summer of 1948 witnessed the briefest of all the Sea Fury commissions, when 806 Squadron was resurrected for a few months in order to take part in a promotional tour of North America, several Sea Furies being accompanied by three Sea Hornets and a Vampire (for the full story of this remarkable excursion, see author Alan Leahy's sister-volume on the Sea Hornet in our 'From the Cockpit' series).

803 Squadron was at this time a Royal Canadian Navy unit, and it was joined in receiving Sea Furies by the RCN's 883 Squadron in September 1948. The next FAA squadron to form on Furies was 804, which was issued with Mk 11s from July 1949, followed by 808 (RAN) in April 1950 and 801 and 898 the following year. Meanwhile 860 Squadron, nominally included in the FAA's roll but in fact a unit of the Royal Netherlands Navy, had begun to receive Sea Fury Mk 50s, which differed from the FAA's Mk 10s only in terms of their communications equipment. The final FAA Sea Fury to commission, in August 1953, was 811, for embarkation on board HMS *Warrior*. The unit was rapidly deployed to the Far East for possible operations off Korea, in the wake of 807, 804, 805, 802 and 801 Squadrons, which hitherto, together with their companion Firefly squadrons, had borne the responsibility of British air operations in the theatre. However, the ceasefire that came into being the previous month held, and the carrier's

presence in Korean waters was not required. The RAN's 850 Squadron was established against the same contingency. Finally, two further Canadian units, 870 and 871 NAS, flew Sea Furies, the former coming about by the renumbering of 803 Squadron in May 1951 and the latter by redesignating 883 Squadron at the same time.

In June 1948 a reorganisation within the Fleet Air Arm saw a change in its aircraft's designation system and a change in the colour schemes carried by its aircraft and the presentation of markings thereon. Roman type designators were abandoned in favour of arabic numerals, and so, for example, the Sea Fury F. Mk X was henceforward officially referred to as the Sea Fury F. Mk 10. From that time also—although the change was neither sudden nor implemented with any particular urgency—FAA fixed-wing combat aircraft adopted a colour scheme of Extra Dark Sea Grey upper surfaces and Sky Type 'S' lower surfaces, the extent of the latter reaching up the fuselage sides and also enveloping the tailfin. The national roundels on wings and fuselage were altered to what is generally referred to as Type 'D', with the central white disc expanded in width, producing a more even distribution of the three colours. Fin flashes were dispensed with.

The overall colour scheme of the Sea Furies prior to the summer of 1948—and, on some aircraft, lingering as a relic for many years after that—was, we are advised in almost all existing reference works, Extra Dark Sea Grey with Sky under surfaces, the former colour extending down to the lower contours of the fuselage. However, it is possible that this is too dogmatic an assurance. Many retired personnel associated with the early days of flying the Sea Fury refer to the aircraft as being 'camouflaged', the clear implication in the context being that later aircraft were 'not camouflaged'. This is a trifle odd if only the demarcation line changed and the shades remained constant. Further, one can tentatively identify, from a study of images of early Sea Furies, traces of camouflage demarcation lines. The difficulty of course is that, in black-and-white photographs, Extra Dark Sea Grey and the other camouflage colour in use during the mid-1940s, Dark Slate Grey, are, tonally, practically indistinguishable—and almost totally indistinguishable if the aircraft paintwork happens to be glossy. Even the few colour photographs of Sea Furies of the era do not provide indisputable proof that no operational Sea Furies wore disruptive camouflage. This is, clearly, a matter for further investigation.

Below: 802 NAS Sea Furies at RNAS Arbroath in the early months of 1953.

SEA FURY

801 NAVAL AIR SQUADRON

Located at RNAS Lee-on-Solent, Ford *et alibi* and on board HM Ships *Implacable*, *Vengeance*, *Indomitable* and *Glory*

Commission: 01/07/47–31/01/55 (Sea Fury Mk 11s 00/03/51–31/01/55, Mk 20s 00/12/51–31/01/55)
Commanding Officers: Lt-Cdr J. G. Baldwin DSC, Lt-Cdr L. T. Summerfield (08/09/51), Lt-Cdr A. Gordon-Johnson (10/12/51), Lt-Cdr P. B. Stuart (01/05/52), Lt-Cdr J. H. S. Pearce DSC (01/03/54)
Senior Pilots: Lt J. H. S. Pearce (1952–54)

Above: 801 Squadron's Sea Furies, with 813's Firebrands, at RNAS Lee-on-Solent, probably in the spring of 1952; see pages 40–41 for another photograph taken at this time. Some of the Sea Furies have had their tail code letter—'A' for HMS *Indomitable*—sprayed over, which suggests that the aircraft may be preparing for their next deployment on board HMS *Glory* ('R').

Below: The Squadron in late 1953 at RNAS Hal Far, following its deployment in combat over Korea. Some of the aircraft are combat veterans—WE709, front row right, for example, tangled with MiGs on one occasion—but all traces of combat markings have been removed and the aircraft are, as in the photograph above, very cleanly presented.

Above: A photograph of the Squadron's personnel taken in late 1952: (front row, left to right) Lieutenants P. D. Handscombe, A. J. Leahy and J. H. S. Pearce (SP), Lieutenant-Commander P. B. Stuart (CO), Cdr B. C. G. Place VC DSC and Lieutenants R. J. McCandless and R. A. Langley (AEO); (centre row, left to right) Sub-Lieutenant D. McL. Baynes, Lieutenants P. A. B. Wemyss, D. G. Mather, P. Wheatley and V. B. Mitchell, and Sub-Lieutenants M. B. Smith, G. B. S. Foster and R. D. Bradley; (back row, left to right) Sub-Lieutenant J. M. Simmonds RNVR, Lieutenants J. F. Fiddian-Green, E. R. Anson and C. A. McPherson, Sub-Lieutenant B. E. Rayner, Lieutenant J. R. T. Bluett, and Sub-Lieutenants J. F. Belville and W. J. B. Keates.

Above: The Squadron at Hal Far, 1953: (front row, left to right) Lieutenants Handscombe, Langdon (AEO) and Pearce (SP), Lieutenant-Commander Stewart (CO), and Lieutenants R. J. McCandless, A. J. Leahy (AWO) and P. Wheatley; (centre row, left to right) Sub-Lieutenant Baynes, Lieutenant J. Bowden, Sub-Lieutenant Foster, and Lieutenants Anson, Mitchell and Fiddian-Green; (back row, left to right) unknown, Sub-Lieutenant Smith, Lieutenants J. A. S. Crawford and Bluett, and Sub-Lieutenants Belville, M. Hayes and A. R. Pearson. Among those missing are Lieutenant McPherson and Sub-Lieutenants Bradley, Keates, Rayner and Simmonds, all, sadly, killed in action over Korea.

Overleaf: Another aerial photograph of 801 Squadron at Hal Far in 1953. The identifying tail letters are much larger than hitherto, and extend across the rudders, and notice, too, that the whip aerials are now standardised in position atop the tailfin.

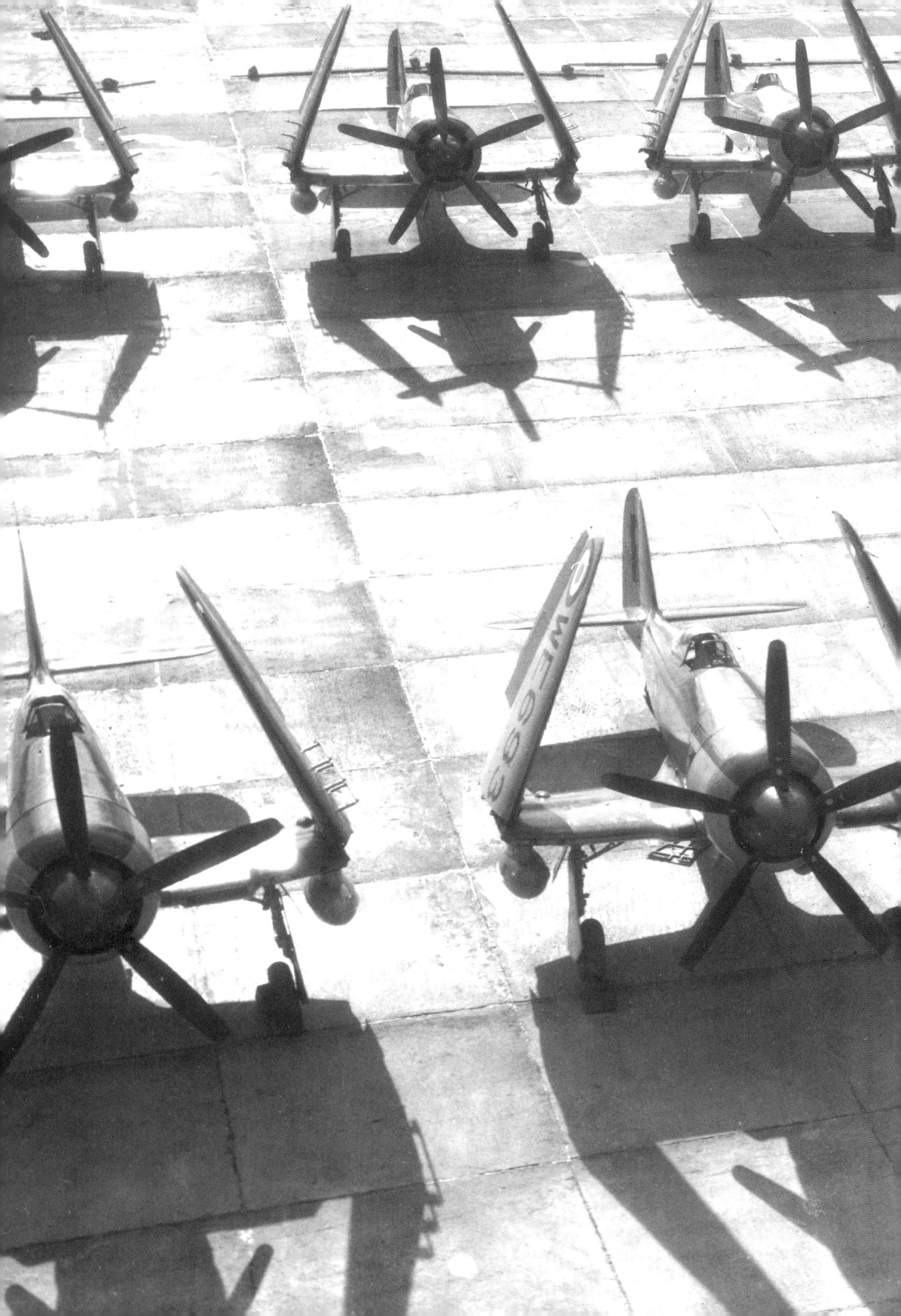

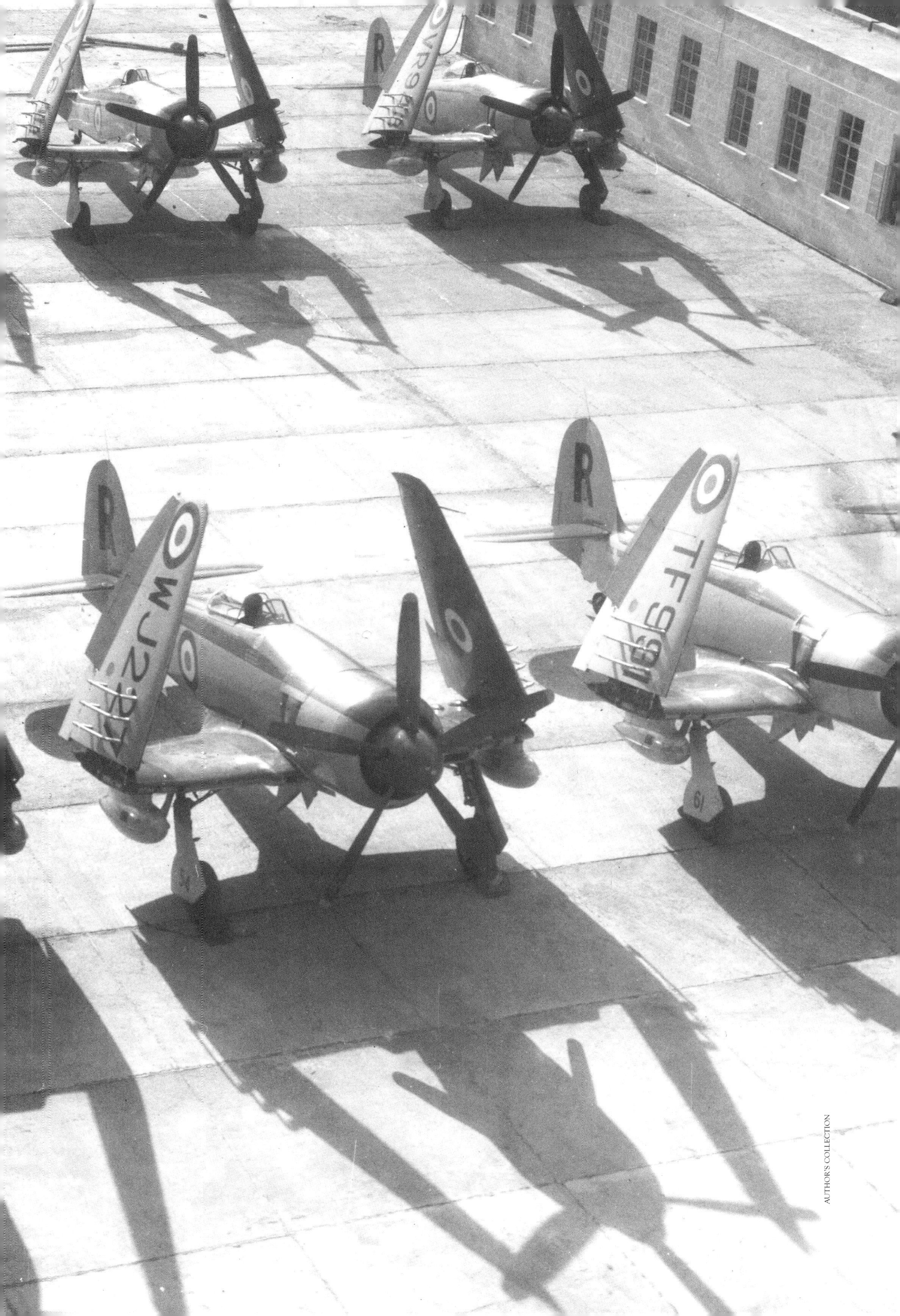

AUTHOR'S COLLECTION

SEA FURY

802 NAVAL AIR SQUADRON

Located at RNAS Lee-on-Solent, Eglinton, Culdrose, Arbroath, Brawdy, Lossiemouth *et alibi* and on board HM Ships *Vengeance* and *Theseus*

Commissions: 01/05/45–10/12/52 and 02/02/53–22/11/55 (Sea Fury Mk 10s 00/04/48–00/06/48, Mk 11s 00/05/48–10/12/52 and 02/02/53–00/03/54, Mk 20s 00/06/50–10/12/52 and 02/02/53–00/02/54)
Commanding Officers: Lt-Cdr M. Horden DSC, Lt-Cdr R. W. Kearsley (22/12/48), Lt-Cdr P. H. Moss (07/04/50), Lt-Cdr J. M. Henry (21/08/50), Lt-Cdr S. F. F. Shotton DSC (21/01/51), Lt-Cdr R. A. Dick DSC (13/07/52), Lt-Cdr P. H. London DSC (14/08/52), Lt-Cdr D. M. Steer (02/02/53), Lt-Cdr I. H. F. Martin DSC (19/08/54)
Senior Pilots: Lt-Cdr P. H. London DSC (c.1950), Lt-Cdr E. M. Brown DSC AFC (in 1951), Lt-Cdr R. A. Dick DSC (1951–12/07/52)

Left: A mishap involving 802 Squadron's Sea Fury F.B.11 VR940, which nosed over after running into the barrier on board HMS *Vengeance*, 17 August 1948. The pilot involved here was none other than Lieutenant-Commander George Baldwin DSC, CO 15th Carrier Air Group, which was made up of the Squadron's Sea Furies and 814 Squadron's co-embarked Fireflies.

Below: Another barrier encounter on the same day, this time involving VR929 of the Squadron. Attempting to land on *Vengeance*, Lieutenant Baillie failed to arrest when his hook bounced off the deck between Nos 6 and 7 wires. Despite immediate impressions here, there is on the original photograph clear evidence of disruptive camouflage demarcation lines, in conformity to the relevant official pattern, especially close to the trailing edge of the starboard wing.

FRONT-LINE SEA FURY SQUADRONS

Above: F.B.11 VW575 in 1950, carrying the new FAA colour scheme and with a miniature rendering of the 802 Squadron crest just ahead of the cockpit windscreen. An FAA Meteor is parked in the distance.

Left: WJ233 caught in the act of exceeding the width of HMS *Ocean*'s flight deck during a landing, June 1952. The aircraft was being delivered to the Squadron from maintenance when this incident occurred and it has yet to receive a tail code and a side number.

Below: WJ280 in pristine finish in 1953, with the Squadron crest displayed on the tailfin.

93

Waterlogged *Commander J. H. ('Boot') Nethersole*

In 1950–51, 802 Squadron was normally land-based at RNAS Culdrose when not at sea, embarked during this commission in HMS *Vengeance* although enjoying short periods also on board *Illustrious*, *Indomitable* and *Implacable*. However, in February 1951 the Dutch Sea Fury squadron, 860, found themselves land-locked because the sole Dutch aircraft carrier, *Karel Doorman*, was being refitted and was thus temporarily *hors de combat*. To help them out, the Admiralty decided that it would offer the Dutch the berth on board *Vengeance* that would otherwise have been occupied by 802. The latter therefore found itself somewhat kicking its heels at Culdrose.

To alleviate any threatened boredom, it was decided to take 802 to Wunsdorf in Germany to put in some hours of army liaison work, and this deployment would be followed by one of a few weeks at RAF Wattisham, for the purposes of getting in some high-altitude interception practice against the American B-29s that regularly plied the East Anglian skies. Sea Fury pilots were generally much more used to low- and medium-altitude flying, and so the chance to climb a few thousand more feet was a new experience for many. I for one will never forget the effects of hitting the slipstream of a large aeroplane at altitude on completion of a camera gun attack! We also managed to fit in a few practice strikes against MTBs in the North Sea.

Wattisham was very welcoming to us in every way except, perhaps, in terms of our hangar allocation. Two of the four hangars in a semi-circle behind the control tower had been bombed during the war and had lost their roofs; the resident Meteor squadrons, naturally enough, occupied the two intact hangars. Although the offices and storerooms along the sides of our roofless hangar were reasonably waterproof and so usable, the hangar floor was three inches below outside ground level, and as it hardly stopped raining while we were there . . . well, one can work it out. Solemnly, however, we nevertheless garaged twelve aircraft in the hangar every night, if only to make a point.

We had some memorable parties in the Mess with the Meteor boys. I recall that one night Wingco Flying punched out the ceiling lights to achieve more of a night-club atmosphere, unfortunately cutting his hand quite badly in the process. There was also the occasion when a prominent and well-known member of the Squadron—none other than our SP, 'Winkle' Brown, in fact!—was hoisted, inverted, to plant his paint-dipped footsteps over the ceiling.

The aerodrome used to organise a weekend bus down to London which I took once, but, having got out before the bus reached its destination at King's Cross, I couldn't find where it was starting its return journey. However, being a keen young officer not wanting to be late back for Monday's flying programme, I borrowed my father's large Humber limo—which came in very useful during the week as we found that we could get all the aircrew in it so as to tour the local hostelries (some extremely good ones, too!).

My logbook tells me that we flew into Wattisham on 15 February 1951 and left to return to Culdrose on 7 March. It was a good visit!

Below: A 'prang' involving F.B.11 VX614 ('180/T') of 802 Squadron, which experienced a hydraulic failure in June 1953 while the pilot, Sub-Lieutenant Randall, was preparing to land at Hal Far, with the result that one of the main undercarriage legs failed to lock. The aircraft was repaired but was not reissued to a squadron.

FRONT-LINE SEA FURY SQUADRONS

803 NAVAL AIR SQUADRON

Located at RNAS Dartmouth, Lee-on-Solent *et alibi* and on board HMCS *Magnificent*

Commission: 15/06/45–01/05/51 (Sea Fury Mk 10s 00/08/47–00/02/50, Mk 11s 00/02/48–01/05/51)
Commanding Officers: Lt-Cdr H. J. G. Bird RCN, Lt-Cdr J. P. Whitby RCN (00/08/48), Lt-Cdr V. J. Wilgress RCN (00/09/48), Lt-Cdr N. Cogdon RCN (14/05/49), Lt-Cdr D. D. Peacocke RCN (15/01/51)
Senior Pilots: Not known

Left: Its squadron crest carried proudly on the engine cowling, VW552 of 803 Squadron, Royal Canadian Navy, rests in the sunshine at NAS Dartmouth. Unlike their FAA brethren, Canadian Sea Furies in the 1950s had their undersurfaces and fuselage sides generally finished in pale grey, and the aircraft retained a red, white and blue flash on the tailfin. On this particular aircraft, the course of the demarcation line at the base of the leading edge of the fin is unusual.

COURTESY PHILIP JARRETT

804 NAVAL AIR SQUADRON

Located at RNAS Hal Far, Brawdy, Lossiemouth *et alibi* and on board HM Ships *Glory* and *Theseus*.

Commission: 01/10/46–17/11/55 (Sea Fury Mk 11s 00/07/49–27/11/53)
Commanding Officers: Lt-Cdr C. F. Hargreaves, Lt-Cdr J. S. Bailey (01/12/50), Lt-Cdr J. R. Routley (23/07/52)
Senior Pilots: Lt-Cdr M. A. Birrell (1951)

Below: Personnel of 804 Squadron in the Mediterranean in early 1951 prior to departure on board HMS *Glory* for Korea: (front row, left to right) Lieutenants R. C. B. Trelawney, W, R. Hart, P. Barlow and D. A. McNaughton, Lieutenant-Commanders R. W. W. Blake (SP 812 NAS), S. J. Hall DSC (AGC), J. S. Bailey OBE (CO) and M. A. Birrell (SP) and Lieutenants R. H. Kilburn, G. W. Bricker, K. Whitaker, J. A. Winterbottom and E. P. L. Stephenson; (back row, left to right) Commissioned Pilots C. E. Mason, D. F. Fieldhouse and M. I. Darlington (?), Pilot 3rd Class R. E. Collingwood and Commissioned Pilots P. O. Richards, F. Hefford and T. Sparke.

COURTESY FRED HEFFORD

95

Above: Rudder damage to 804 Squadron's VW703, CO Lieutenant-Commander Bill Bailey's aircraft, brought about during the course of duties in Korean waters between June and October 1951 when it was struck by another that had been unable to stop after landing-on because its port brake had been hit by anti-aircraft fire.

Below: 804 Squadron personnel on or soon after 6 February 1952, wearing black armbands to mark the passing of HM King George VI: (front row, left to right) Lieutenants A. G. Cordell (RAN), P. S. Davis, K. Whitaker and J. R. Fraser (SP), Lieutenant-Commander J. S. Bailey OBE (CC), and Lieutenants D. A. McNaughton, P. Barlow and P. I. Normand; (centre row, left to right) Commissioned Pilot B. J. Potts, Sub-Lieutenant C. E. Haines, Commissioned Pilots M. I. Darlington, W. A. Newton, F. Hefford and D. F. Fieldhouse and Sub-Lieutenant P. H. Wyatt (RAN); (back row, left to right) Sub-Lieutenants J. R. Howard, D. K. G. Swanson and A. G. Fowell (RAN) and Commissioned Pilot R. E. Collingwood.

Above: A late-production Sea Fury in the colours of 804 Naval Air Squadron, embellished with the Squadron crest on the tailfin, a red and white spinner and a red-shanked arrester hook, at RNAS Brawdy in 1953.

The Sea Fury's days in the front-line squadrons were now numbered: by the end of the year 804 would be taking delivery of its elegant jet-powered successor, the Sea Hawk.

805 NAVAL AIR SQUADRON

Located at RNAS Eglinton and NAS Nowra and on board HMAS *Sydney*

Commission: 28/08/48–26/03/58 (Sea Fury Mk 10s 28/08/48–00/02/49, Mk 11s throughout)
Commanding Officers: Lt-Cdr P. E. Bailey, Lt-Cdr C. J. Cunningham DSC (11/11/49), Lt-Cdr W. G. Bowles (05/04/50), Lt-Cdr J. R. N. Salthouse RAN (09/04/51), Lt-Cdr G. Jude RAN (28/01/52), Lt-Cdr D. R. Hare RAN (08/04/52), Lt-Cdr G. F. S. Brown RAN (11/08/52), Lt-Cdr N. R. Williams RAN (19/04/53), Lt-Cdr A. J. Gould RAN (20/05/53), Lt-Cdr J. T. Sherborne RAN (26/07/54), Lt-Cdr R. E. Bourke RAN (03/05/55), Lt-Cdr J. G. B. Campbell DSC RAN (26/11/56), Lt-Cdr B. Stock RAN (28/02/58)
Senior Pilots: Not known

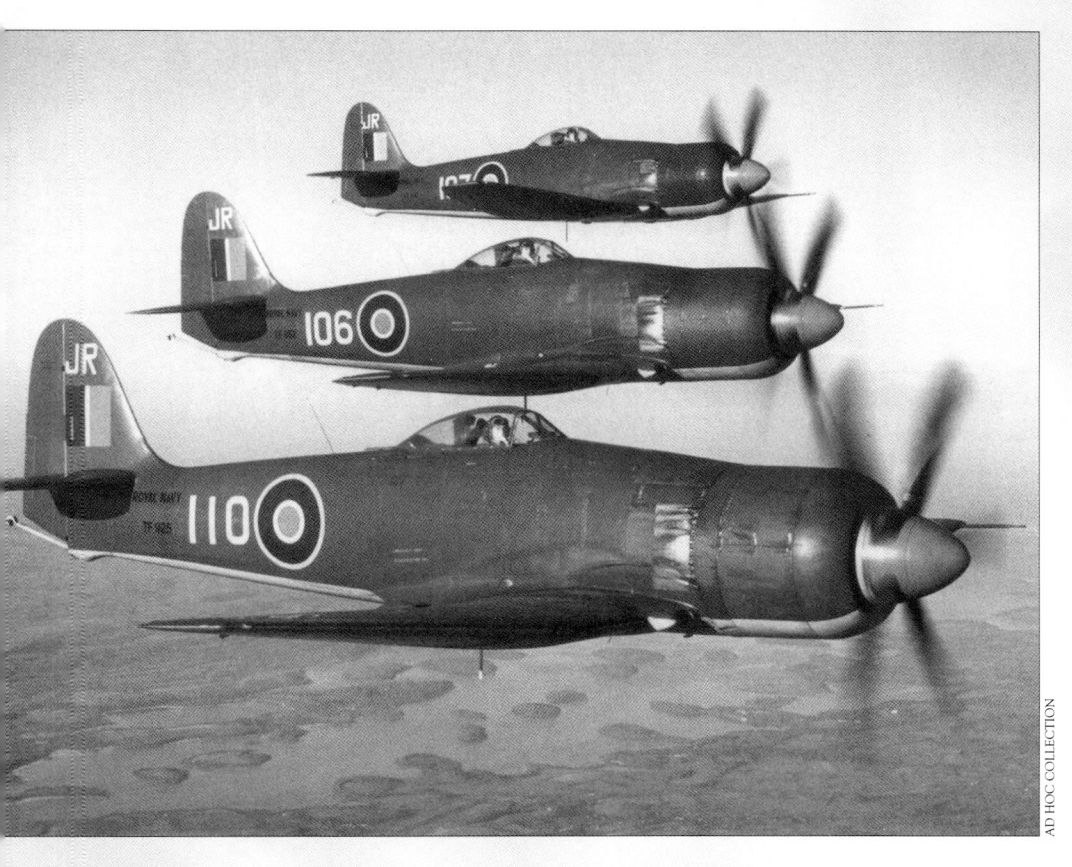

Left: A well-known photograph of a trio of 805 Squadron Sea Furies, comprising TF925, TF952 and VR950. The two nearest aircraft are Mk 10s and the furthest a Mk 11. The tail code 'JR' signifies RNAS Eglinton in Northern Ireland, where the Squadron was based before embarking on board the aircraft carrier HMAS *Sydney* for passage to Australia. Although the upper surfaces of these aircraft are, apparently, finished in an overall Extra Dark Sea Grey, it is, again, possible in the original prints to make out what appear to be disruptive patterns in places. The propeller spinners are painted red.

97

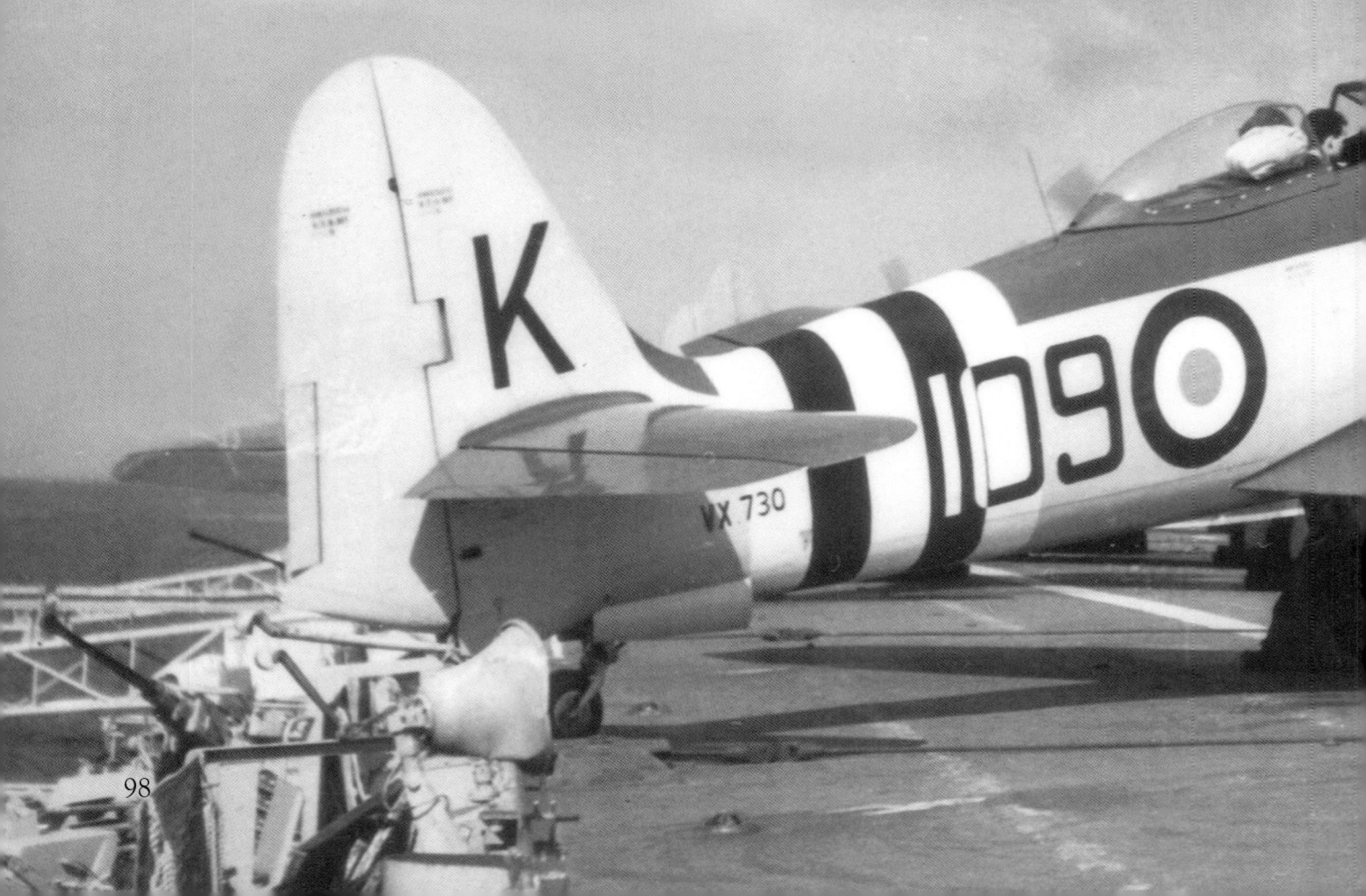

SEA FURY

FRONT-LINE SEA FURY SQUADRONS

Main image: A scene on board HMAS *Sydney* in autumn 1951, just prior to the carrier's deployment for combat operations off Korea. The aircraft depicted, 805 Squadron's VX730, is still in existence, preserved as part of the Australian War Memorial in Canberra.

Left, upper: VW638 of 805 Squadron at NAS Bankstown after the Korean War. The rudder is turned to starboard and in shadow, giving the appearance of its being painted in a dark colour.

Left, lower: In July 1956 the Royal Australian Air Force and Royal Australian Navy introduced a revised system of presentation for military aircraft markings, a red kangaroo replacing the central disc in the roundel and the tenancy and individual aircraft number of each aircraft now proclaimed large along the fuselage sides. The new styling is exemplified here by 805 Squadron's Sea Fury WH587.

806 NAVAL AIR SQUADRON

Located at NAS Dartmouth (see captions)

Commissions: 03/05/48–25/09/48 (Sea Fury Mk 11s throughout)
Commanding Officer: Lt-Cdr D. B. Law DSC
Senior Pilot: Lt A. B. B. Clark

Above: Pilots and aircraft of the diminutive 806 Squadron in the summer of 1948. The unit was established with the specific task of forming an aerobatic display team for presentation in North America, a tour that culminated in much-praised performances at the ceremonial opening of New York International Airport (otherwise known as Idlewild Airport and now named John F. Kennedy Airport) from 31 July to 8 August that year. The four Sea Furies in the team are furthest from view. The pilots are (left to right) Lieutenants D. H. Reynolds DSC, J. C. Sloan (RCN) and F. G. Rice (RCN), Lieutenant-Commander D. B. Law DSC (CO) and Lieutenants A. B. B. Clark (SP) and I. H. F. Martin DSC.

Below: The Sea Furies of 806 Squadron were drawn from a small pool comprising VR934 (left at Eglinton owing to engine problems), VR944, VR932, TG124 (another replacement, and an RCN Fury), TG113 (RCN) and TG127 (RCN)—all F. B. Mk 11s. Here VR932 and TG124 bring up the rear as the team taxies in after a display. Barely visible behind TG124's starboard undercarriage leg is D. H. Vampire VF515, also part of the Squadron.

FRONT-LINE SEA FURY SQUADRONS

807 NAVAL AIR SQUADRON

Located at NAS Eglinton, Culdrose, Lee-on-Solent, Hal Far, Yeovilton *et alibi* and on board HM Ships *Theseus*, *Ocean* and *Glory*

Commissions: 15/09/40–04/11/55 (Sea Fury Mk 10s 00/09/47–00/12/48, Mk 11s 00/02/48–00/05/54)
Commanding Officers: Lt-Cdr S. J. Hall, Lt-Cdr W. N. Waller (13/04/48), Lt-Cdr A. J. Thomson DSC (08/07/48), Lt-Cdr M. P. Gordon-Smith DSC (25/07/49), Lt-Cdr B. Bevans (00/01/51), Lt-Cdr A. J. Thomson DSC (15/06/51), Lt-Cdr T. L. M. Brander DSC (01/01/53), Lt-Cdr P. J. Hutton DSC (14/01/54)
Senior Pilots: Lt-Cdr B. Bevans (in 1950)

Above: The aftermath of an unhappy landing by Sea Fury Mk 11 WG600 on HMS *Ocean* on 18 August 1951, from which the pilot, Sub-Lieutenant A. J. Austin, emerged unscathed despite the fact that the aircraft caught fire.

Below: A tailless WF590 of the Squadron is salvaged following its inversion as the result of a crash landing on board *Ocean* in August 1953; again the pilot, this time Dutchman Lieutenant A. H. M. Hagdorn, escaped unhurt.

101

808 NAVAL AIR SQUADRON

Located at RNAS St Merryn and NAS Nowra and on board HMAS *Sydney* and *Vengeance*

Commission: 25/04/50–05/10/54 (Sea Fury Mk 11s throughout)
Commanding Officers: Lt-Cdr J. L. Appleby RAN, Lt-Cdr J. H. G. Cavanagh RAN (20/07/52), Lt-Cdr G. A. Beange DSC (18/05/53)
Senior Pilots: Not known

Left: 808 NAS recommissioned as a Royal Australian Navy squadron on April 1950, equipped with Sea Furies for service with 805 Squadron, and 817 Squadron's Fireflies, on board HMAS *Sydney*. It saw action off Korea with these units during the autumn and winter of 1951. This aircraft, VX707, was allocated to 808 but remained in reserve during the conflict.

809 NAVAL AIR SQUADRON

Located at RNAS Culdrose

Commission: 20/01/49–10/05/54 (one Sea Fury Mk 20 00/11/51–00/01/52)
Commanding Officer: Lt-Cdr D. H. Richards
Senior Pilots: Not known

810 NAVAL AIR SQUADRON

Located at RNAS Ford and Hal Far and on board HMS *Centaur*

Commission: 01/03/54–22/03/55 (Sea Fury Mk 11s throughout)
Commanding Officer: Lt-Cdr H. J. Abraham
Senior Pilots: Not known

Left: 810 Squadron's existence as a Sea Fury unit was both sudden and brief: it re-formed in March 1953 having previously been a Firefly unit, as which it had seen action as the shipmate of 807 Squadron off Korea. It was embarked on board the new light fleet carrier *Centaur* but after twelve months was disbanded pending the arrival of Sea Hawk jets. The black identifying markings carried by 810's Sea Furies were notably bold in character. This example, WE693, had lately served with 801 Squadron, the overpainted tail code letter for that unit's parent ship, *Glory*, being readily apparent.

FRONT-LINE SEA FURY SQUADRONS

811 NAVAL AIR SQUADRON

Located at RNAS Arbroath, RAF Leuchars, RNAS Lee-on-Solent *et alibi* and on board HMS *Warrior*

Commission: 17/08/53–30/12/54 (Sea Fury Mk 11s throughout)
Commanding Officer: Lt-Cdr L. G. Morris
Senior Pilots: Not known

Above: 811 NAS was another fairly short-lived Sea Fury unit: it was re-formed as a contingency against the continuation of the Korean War, but, in the event, hostilities ceased a few weeks before its recommissioning. The tail letter 'J' at the time denoted HMS *Warrior* and was shared with aircraft embarked on the big fleet carrier HMS *Eagle*.

Below: A safety barrier is disentangled from WG599 of 811 Squadron following a 'bounced' landing on board *Warrior*, June 1954. It must be emphasised that the ubiquity of photographs relating to deck-landing accidents is not the result of any sort of voyeurism: such images are an invaluable resource in the continuing resolve to improve safety at sea.

103

SEA FURY

850 NAVAL AIR SQUADRON

Located at NAS Nowra and on board HMAS *Vengeance* and *Sydney*

Commission: 12/01/53–03/08/54 (Sea Fury Mk 11s throughout)
Commanding Officers: Lt-Cdr R. A. Wilde DFC, Lt-Cdr P. M. Austin (18/05/53)
Senior Pilots: Not known

Left: VX758, seen here looking somewhat anonymous, served with the RAN's 850 Squadron throughout most of its career. The fuselage top panel behind the engine has been removed—perhaps preparatory to the type of percussive maintenance described by the author on page 70!

COURTESY RICHARD L. WARD

860 NAVAL AIR SQUADRON

Located at RNAS St Merryn, RNNAS Valkenburg and on board HrMS *Karel Doorman*

Commission: 15/07/50–15/06/56 (Sea Fury Mk 50s throughout)
Commanding Officers: Not known
Senior Pilots: Not known.

Below: The *Koninklijke Marine*—Royal Netherlands Navy—received a number of Sea Fury Mk 50s for service in the front line with 860 Squadron, a Dutch unit that, in its designation, maintained its wartime links with the FAA for some years afterwards. This aircraft, coded '10-2', is seen at Hawker's Langley Airfield, ready for delivery to its owners. In external configuration, the early Dutch Sea Furies were indistinguishable from the Mk 10s of the Royal Navy.

COURTESY TONY BUTTLER

104

Above: In line with their FAA counterparts, Dutch Sea Furies adopted the new FAA colour scheme quite soon after entering service, as exemplified here by '8-39', part of a second batch of aircraft designated Mk 60 (equivalent to the Mk 11). The individual aircraft numbers were repeated on the engine cowling.

Below: The Dutch experienced their fair share of landing mishaps, as here on board HrMS *Karel Doorman* in 1953. This accident resulted in a rather nasty conflagration as the aircraft met the barrier, although, fortunately, the cockpit has been vacated—as shown dramatically in one of the photographs on the back cover of this book.

SEA FURY

870 NAVAL AIR SQUADRON

Located at NAS Dartmouth, Summerside *et alibi* and on board HMCS *Magnificent*

Commission: 01/05/51–30/03/54 (Sea Fury Mk 11s throughout)
Commanding Officers: Lt-Cdr D. D. Peacocke RCN, Lt-Cdr D. M. McLeod RCN (09/02/53)
Senior Pilots: Not known

871 NAVAL AIR SQUADRON

Located at NAS Dartmouth and on board HMCS *Magnificent*

Commission: 01/05/51–16/03/59 (Sea Fury Mk 11s 01/05/51–00/08/56)
Commanding Officers: Lt-Cdr W. D. Munro RCN, Lt-Cdr D. H. P. Ryan RCN (00/11/51), Lt-Cdr R. Heath RCN (00/07/52), Lt-Cdr M. Wasteneys RCN (23/03/53), Lt-Cdr J. W. Logan RCN (02/07/54), Lt-Cdr R. A. Laidsler RCN (13/01/56)
Senior Pilots: Not known

883 NAVAL AIR SQUADRON

Located at NAS Dartmouth and on board HMCS *Magnificent*

Commission: 15/05/47–01/05/51 (Sea Fury Mk 11s 00/09/48–01/05/51)
Commanding Officers: Lt-Cdr J. B. Fotheringham RCN, Lt-Cdr R. A. B. Creery RCN (01/12/48), Lt-Cdr W. D. Munro RCN (00/04/50)
Senior Pilots: Not known

Right, upper: Two further Canadian Sea Fury squadrons were commissioned during the 1950s, although they were not entirely separate entities: 870 was established by means of renumbering 803 (see page 95), while 871 was formed the same day that 883 Squadron was disbanded, taking over many of the latter's aircraft in the process. This photograph shows VW231, in service with 871 Squadron.

Right, lower: Like the Royal Australian Navy, the RCN revised the presentation of its markings in the mid-1950s, opting for something altogether more striking than that pertaining hitherto—as seen both in the previous photograph and here on WG572, in service, as depicted, with 871 Squadron in 1956. At about this time also, Canadian naval units adopted the US system of designation, so that 870 Squadron was henceforth known as VF-870, 871 Squadron as VF-871, and so on. RCN Sea Furies went to sea on board two ships, HMS *Warrior*, temporarily taken into service from 1946 to 1948, and then HMS *Magnificent*, another of the very successful British-built *Majestic* class light fleet carriers.

FRONT-LINE SEA FURY SQUADRONS

898 NAVAL AIR SQUADRON

Located at RNAS Arbroath and Hal Far and on board HMS *Ocean*, *Theseus* and *Glory*

Commission: 04/07/51–19/04/56 (Sea Fury Mk 11s 04/07/51–00/01/53)
Commanding Officer: Lt-Cdr D. G. Parker DSO DSC DFC
Senior Pilots: Not known

Above: Wind-over-deck, v. 2.0. During periods of aircraft launch and recovery, carriers generate wind-over-deck by steaming at speed into whatever natural wind may be available, in order to offer the pilots the best possible conditions for lift, thereby minimising take-off and landing runs. This photograph depicts something called 'pinwheeling': wind-over-deck is being generated, but here by means of the Furies running their engines and creating sufficient draught to help their ship—HMS *Ocean*—to manœuvre in Grand Harbour, Valletta.
Left, upper: A list to starboard for 898 Squadron's Sea Fury WF621 following a collision on board *Ocean* with a Firefly, resulting in the collapse of an undercarriage leg and a visit to the repair shop.
Left, lower: Another photograph of 898 Squadron's WE693 (see page 28) following its deck-landing accident on 11 December 1952. The aircraft is interesting in that whereas the starboard wing is painted with Korean-era black and white recognition stripes, the port wing—or, at least, its upper surface—is not
Overleaf: 898 and 810 (Firefly) Squadrons on board *Theseus* in the Mediterranean in autumn 1952. The aircraft are wearing temporary markings unrelated to those adopted for the Korean conflict.

107

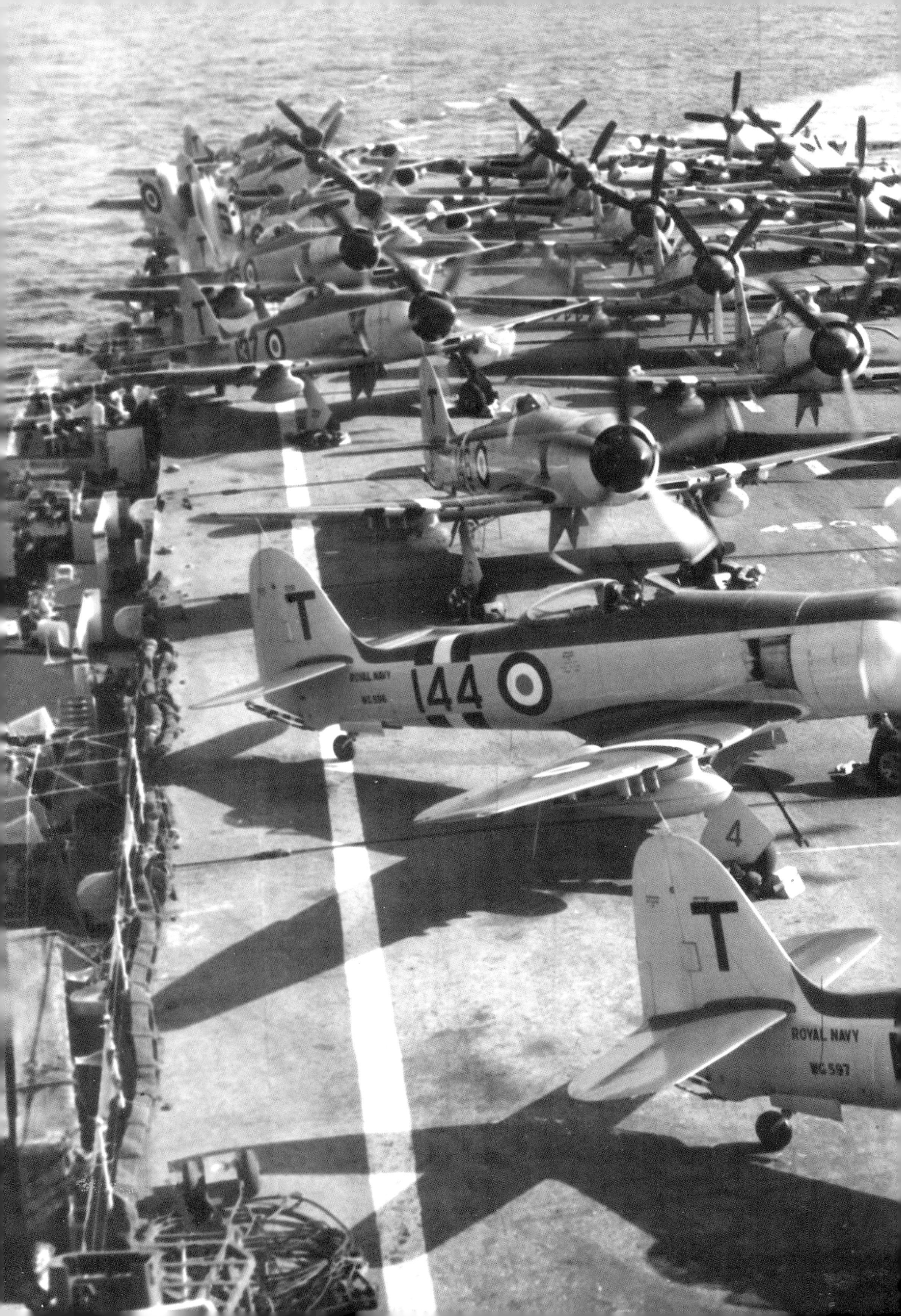
T
144
T
ROYAL NAVY
WG 597

COURTESY MICHAEL DOUST

RNVR SEA FURY SQUADRONS

FORMALLY established in 1938, the Air Branch of the Royal Naval Volunteer Reserve provided the Fleet Air Arm with a pool of highly qualified civilian aviators upon which it could call in the event of emergency; indeed, many thousands of the officers and airmen flying with the Fleet Air Arm during World War II were RNVR personnel. In 1948 the Air Branch was restricted in its complement to fighter and anti-submarine aircraft, and in 1957 it was disestablished as part of the cuts imposed by the Defence Review of that year.

A variety of aircraft were flown by RNVR personnel in the postwar years, and these were types that had already been serving with the front-line squadrons for some years and, though not necessarily 'second-hand', were deemed surplus to front-line requirements. Fighter squadrons were numbered in the 1830 series and anti-submarine units—generally operating marks of Firefly—in the 1840 series. From 1951 onwards the Sea Fury was issued to the Northern (Stretton), Midland (Bramcote) and Southern (Culham, then Benson and Yeovilton) Air Divisions of the RNVR, replacing the late-mark Supermarine Seafires with which they had hitherto been equipped.

Commanded by very experienced Naval officers, RNVR volunteers were drawn from all walks of life and were jocularly—and not entirely inaccurately—referred to as 'Weekend Warriors'. There was a regular, annual Summer Camp—usually taking place at a front-line Naval Air Station (which might, for the fortunate, prove to be RNAS Hal Far in Malta)—and the opportunity was afforded to RNVR aviators to undertake some deck landing training whenever a carrier could be spared for the purpose.

The contribution made by the RNVR, often mentioned only in passing by historians, was immense—and those who joined will confirm that without exception they both relished the experience and benefited from it.

Above: The RNVR fighter units operated both single- and two-seat Furies. This is a T.20 assigned to 1833 Squadron at Bramcote.

Below: With a marshal in his sights, Lieutenant-Commander David Jenkins, CO of 1833 Squadron, taxies back to dispersal after a rocket-firing sortie in his Sea Fury F.B.11 at RNAS Hal Far, September 1954. Three R/P rails beneath each wing was a fit commonly seen on RNVR Furies, especially during Annual Training when a rare opportunity to 'go live' was provided. This aircraft, WZ655, was the penultimate Sea Fury to roll off the production line at Langley.

SEA FURY

1830 NAVAL AIR SQUADRON

Located at RNAS Donibristle, Abbotsinch and Culham

Commission: 15/08/47–10/03/57 (at least one Sea Fury Mk 20 00/10/52–00/10/54)
Commanding Officer: Lt-Cdr R. C. Read RNVR
Senior Pilots: Not known

1831 NAVAL AIR SQUADRON

Located at RNAS Stretton

Commission: 01/06/47–10/03/57 (Sea Fury Mk 11s 00/08/51–00/06/55, Mk 20s 00/10/50–00/06/55)
Commanding Officers: Lt-Cdr R. I. Gilchrist MBE RNVR, Lt-Cdr K. H. Tickle RNVR (01/06/52), Lt-Cdr W. A. Storey RNVR (18/08/52), Lt-Cdr F. Morrell RNVR (00/00/54), Lt-Cdr P. L. V. Rougier RNVR (23/04/55)
Senior Pilots: Not known

Above: VW703 of 1831 Squadron in late 1953 or early 1954, sporting its RNAS Stretton tail code and a dashing, yellow-striped propeller spinner. A Sabre jet is glimpsed in the background.

Left: When the time came for some RNVR deck-landing practice, things did not always go according to plan. VR926, for example came a cropper when landing on board HMS *Illustrious* in June 1953, the cause a failed arrester wire. The pilot, Lieutenant T. J. Hamer of 1831 Squadron, was slightly hurt.

112

RNVR SEA FURY SQUADRONS

1832 NAVAL AIR SQUADRON

Located at RNAS Culham and RAF Benson

Commission: 01/07/47–10/03/57 (Sea Fury Mk 11s 00/08/51–00/08/55, Mk 20s 00/10/50–00/06/56)
Commanding Officers: Lt-Cdr P. Godfrey OBE RNVR, Lt-Cdr G. M. Rutherford MBE DSC RNVR (01/02/52), Lt-Cdr G. R. Willcocks DSC RNVR (01/06/52), Lt-Cdr M. R. H. Shippey RNVR (27/11/53), Lt-Cdr T. C. Fletcher RNVR (30/09/55)
Senior Pilots: Not known

1833 NAVAL AIR SQUADRON

Located at RNAS Bramcote

Commission: 15/08/47–10/03/57 (Sea Fury Mk 11s 00/02/54–00/07/55, Mk 20s 00/10/50–22/10/55)
Commanding Officers: Lt-Cdr R. F. Hallam RNVR, Lt-Cdr B. W. Vigrass RNVR (01/04/52), Lt-Cdr D. G. Jenkins DFC RNVR (28/06/53)
Senior Pilot: Lt-Cdr D. T. Chute

1834 NAVAL AIR SQUADRON

Located at RNAS Benson and Yeovilton

Commission: 10/10/55–30/04/55 (Sea Fury Mk 11s and Mk 20s throughout)
Commanding Officer: Lt-Cdr A. C. B. Ford VRD DSC RNVR
Senior Pilots: Not known

Above: Even familiarity with RATOG was on the curriculum for RNVR pilots, as demonstrated here by a Southern Air Division Sea Fury, VR555.

Right: The RNVR Deck Landing Course at RNAS Ford, July 1954: (seated, left to right) Sub-Lieutenants John Grierson and Alan Bryce, Lieutenant David Farrand, Lieutenant-Commander Derek Fuller (CFI), Lietenant Harry Burman (DLCO), Lieutenant Bill Roper and Sub-Lieutenants Peter Nicholson and Bill Box; (standing, left to right) Sub-Lieutenants Bob Jones, Jim Hopkins, Dick Perry, Ernie Jackson and Peter Taylor. The RNVR officers are distinguishable by their rank insignia—now a 'V' within the executive curl, which replaced the famous 'Wavy Navy' insignia in 1952.

SECOND-LINE SEA FURY SQUADRONS

SECOND-line squadrons—numbered in the Fleet Air Arm in the '700' series—may not be accorded the glamorous status of their front-line brethren, but their work is fundamental. It is these squadrons that rigorously test new aircraft types, to make sure that they are fully compatible with the Navy's requirements; continue to conduct trials to ensure that the aircraft are kept in line with new technologies and equipment; train 'green' aircrews to fit them for service in the front-line squadrons, in terms of both their flying skills and their specialised rôles; provide refresher courses for those in need of them; and to act as repositories for aircraft and crews acting in support and general duties.

Postwar, the largest and most active second-line squadrons have been 736 and 738—during the early 1950s jointly referred to as the Naval Air Fighter School—where fighter pilots were trained in, respectively, airmanship and weaponry. Each squadron might number fifty or more aircraft, with at least that number of personnel in training, at any given time. Every Royal Navy Sea Fury pilot would have had some association with the NAFS at some point in his career.

Left: Sea Fury Mk 11 VW583 ('096/FD') folds its wings as it taxies forward on board HMS *Illustrious*, circa 1954. It is assigned to 703 Squadron, the principal task of which at this time was the proving of catapult and arrester gear on board carriers.
Right: VX608 of 703 Squadron photographed in about 1953 and displaying an unusual style of figure '8' in its side number. The aircraft is equipped with a dummy 1,000-pound bomb on its port wing mounting and there are also what appear to be R/P rails lying casually beneath the wing in long grass, but this image was clearly taken on a public day and in any case 703 did not concern itself a great deal with weaponry.

Unit	Location(s)	Commission(s)
700 NAS	RNAS Yeovilton (1948-49) and Ford (1955-56)	11/10/44-30/09/49 and 18/08/55-03/07/61 (Sea Fury Mk 10s 00/06/48-00/09/49, Mk 11s 00/12/55-00/01/56)
703 NAS	RNAS Lee-on-Solent and Ford	19/04/45-17/08/55 (Sea Fury Mk 10s 00/06/48-00/02/52, Mk 11s 00/07/48-00/03/55, Mk 20s 00/06/51-00/10/51)
723 NAS	NAS Nowra	07/04/52-29/10/56 (Sea Fury Mk 11s throughout)
724 NAS	NAS Nowra	01/06/55-30/06/84 (Sea Fury Mk 11s 01/06/55-00/10/56, 00/05/61-00/10/62)
725 NAS	NAS Nowra	13/01/58-31/05/61 (Sea Fury Mk 11s until 00/05/59)

As vital, and responsible for the efficiency and effectiveness of the aircraft itself, were the trials units. Of these, arguably the most significant in the Sea Fury era were 703, otherwise known as the Service Trials Unit, where aircraft were put through their paces just prior to entering service in the front line, to ensure that all last-minute 'foibles' were identified, analysed and, where possible, corrected; and 787, where, amongst other tasks, fighter tactics were fully explored and recommendations made as a result (and, usually, where the all-important Pilot's Notes were compiled).

As important, though less urgently employed, were the many second-line units acting in a rôle that might be described as continuing support—for example 767, where Aerodrome Dummy Deck Landings (ADDLs) were practised and 'batsmen' were trained in their vital duties. Several other squadrons employed small numbers of Sea Furies, either single-seaters or two-seaters, or both, on a more irregular basis, for such tasks as examining, instrument development, electronic counter-measures research and evaluation, and general communications.

Commanding Officer(s)	Remarks
Lt R. M. Orr-Ewing, Lt W. J. Lovell (18/02/49); Lt-Cdr R. W. Turral (18/08/55)	Maintenance Test Pilot Training Squadron (50th Air Training Group 1948–49); Trials & Requirements Unit 1955–57.
Lt-Cdr W. R. J. McWhirter DSC, Lt-Cdr N. A. Bartlett (08/05/50), Lt-Cdr J. M. Glaser DSC (25/04/51), Lt-Cdr S. M. de L. Longsden (08/01/53), Lt-Cdr F. J. Sherborne (20/07/53), Lt-Cdr J. R. N. Gardner DSC (04/09/53)	Service Trials Unit (and, until 1950, Air–Sea Warfare Development Unit).
Lt-Cdr J. A. Gledhill RAN, Lt-Cdr J. C. B. Campbell DSC RAN (00/04/53), Lt-Cdr G. A. Beange DSC RAN (01/05/53), Lt-Cdr C. M. A. Wheatley RAN (23/05/55)	Fleet requirements and general duties unit.
Lt-Cdr L. A. Robinson RAN (until 1957); Lt-Cdr N. E. Lee RAN (03/02/61), Lt-Cdr A. E. Payne RAN (01/06/61), Lt-Cdr J. P. van Gelder RAN (22/06/62)	Miscellaneous Air Squadron (operational training and aircrew conversion).
Lt-Cdr J. M. Wade-Brown RAN, Lt-Cdr K. M. Barnett RAN (04/08/58)	Fleet Requirements and Communications Unit.

continued . . .

SEA FURY

736 NAS	RNAS St Merryn and Culdrose	24/05/43–26/03/65 (Sea Fury Mk 10s 00/08/50–00/09/51, Mk 11s 00/05/49–00/08/52, Mk 20s 00/03/50–00/08/52)
738 NAS	RNAS Culdrose and Lossiemouth	01/05/50–08/05/70 (Sea Fury Mk 10s 01/05/50–00/08/51, Mk 11s and Mk 20s 01/05/50–00/03/55)
739 NAS	RNAS Culham	01/05/47–12/07/50 (at least one Sea Fury Mk 11 00/09/48–00/09/48)
744 NAS	RNAS Culdrose and RAF St Mawgan	01/03/54–31/10/56 (at least one Sea Fury Mk 11 from 00/05/54)
751 NAS	RAF Watton	03/12/51–01/05/58 (Sea Fury Mk 11s 00/08/52–00/03/56)
759 NAS	RNAS Culdrose and Lossiemouth	16/08/51–12/10/54 (Sea Fury Mk 11s 00/05/52–00/06/52, Mk 20s 00/02/52–00/01/54)
766 NAS	RNAS Lossiemouth	15/04/42–25/11/54 (Sea Fury Mk 20s 00/09/51–00/07/52)
767 NAS	RNAS Yeovilton and Henstridge	24/05/39–31/03/55 (Sea Fury Mk 11s 00/11/49–00/06/52)

Above: St Merryn-based aircraft were identified by the tail code letters 'JB', and this Mk 11 was serving with 736 Squadron when photographed here in 1949. The Squadron crest is borne on the engine cowling.

Right: Sea Fury T. Mk 20 VX297 of 736 Squadron prepares for a solo flight at Culdrose. Alongside can be glimpsed a Supermarine Attacker—the Royal Navy's first jet fighter and the Sea Fury's replacement on the Squadron. The changeover took place in August 1952, offering a probable date for this photograph.

Lt-Cdr M. F. Fell DSO DSC, Lt-Cdr P. J. P. Leckie (05/09/49), Lt-Cdr P. B. Stuart (01/02/50), Lt-Cdr P. M. Austin (17/10/50), Lt-Cdr P. H. London DSC (24/03/52)	Naval Air Fighter School (flying training).
Lt-Cdr S. F. F. Shotton, Lt-Cdr S. A. Mearns DSC (19/01/51), Lt-Cdr H. J. Abraham (12/07/51), Lt-Cdr J. Robertson (03/04/54), Lt-Cdr H. Kenworthy (05/04/54), Lt-Cdr P. Carmichael (28/09/54), Lt-Cdr D. B. Morrison (05/01/55)	Naval Air Fighter School (weapons training).
Lt-Cdr B. A. MacCaw DSC	Photographic Development Unit. One Sea Fury briefly on strength.
Lt-Cdr F. J. G. Arnold, Lt-Cdr R. Fulton (04/01/56)	Naval Air–Sea Warfare Development Unit. At least one Sea Fury allocated.
Lt-Cdr G. R. Woolston, Lt-Cdr W. J. Cooper (02/06/54)	Radio Warfare Unit (electronic countermeasures). Part of Central Signals Establishment.
Lt-Cdr R. D. Lygo, Lt-Cdr D. R. O. Price (30/05/53)	No 1 Operational Flying School. Part of Naval Air Fighter School.
Lt-Cdr J. M. Henry, Lt-Cdr D. W. Winterton (02/12/62)	Operational Flying School Part I.
Lt-Cdr W. E. Simpson, Lt-Cdr C. K. Roberts (19/04/50), Lt-Cdr M. E. Stanley (18/01/51), Lt-Cdr D. O'D Newberry (03/09/51)	Deck landing and DLCO ('batsman') training.

continued . . .

Above: 766 Squadron, host unit for courses associated with Part I of the Operational Flying School, operated a small number of Fury trainers in 1951–52, for example VX300, seen here during an Air Day. The T.20s were invariably finished in silver.

Right: Before a Naval pilot could land on board a carrier he first had to prove—relentlessly—that he could achieve the required approach, and obey the batting signals he was given, on dry land. Facilities for these skills were the preserve of 767 Squadron, based at Yeovilton and nearby Henstridge. Aircraft wheeling round and round in practice landings gave rise to the nickname 'Clockwork Mice'. This is one of them, TF903.

SEA FURY

771 NAS	RNAS Lee-on-Solent	24/05/39-17/08/55 (Sea Fury Mk 20s 00/07/50-00/12/50)
773 NAS	RNAS Lee-on-Solent and RAF North Front	06/01/49-31/03/49 (Sea Fury Mk 11s throughout)
778 NAS	RNAS Ford and Lee-on-Solent	28/09/39-16/08/48 (Sea Fury Mk 10s 00/02/47-00/07/47, Mk 11s 00/02/48-00/08/48)
781 NAS	RNAS Lee-on-Solent	27/06/46-31/03/81 (Sea Fury Mk 10s 00/10/48-00/01/50, Mk 11s 00/12/53-00/02/55, Mk 20s 00/05/50-00/09/54)
782 NAS	RNAS Donibristle	01/12/40-09/10/53 (Sea Fury Mk 11s 00/06/48-00/06/50, Mk 20s 00/05/51-00/10/51)
787 NAS	RAF West Raynham	05/03/41-16/01/56 (Sea Fury Mk 10s 00/05/47-00/07/48, Mk 11s 00/02/49-00/00/54, Mk 20s 00/00/49-00/00/49)
799 NAS	RNAS Yeovilton	30/07/45-12/08/52 (Sea Fury Mk 10s 00/09/48-00/10/49, Mk 11s 00/05/49-00/11/51, Mk 20s 00/04/51-00/05/51)
Station Flights	RNAS Arbroath, Culdrose, Eglinton, Ford, Lossiemouth, St Merryn and Hal Far	Various
Fleet Requirements Unit	Hurn Airport	Sea Fury Mk 11s operated 00/10/55-00/04/61

Left: T.20 VX289, uncoded, served for most of its career with 771 Squadron (which from 1952 was known as the Southern Fleet Requirements Unit). Like that of many other second-line Sea Furies, its work was humdrum but vital. Below: Prior to August 1948, service trials were conducted by 778 Squadron as well as by 703, into which the former was absorbed at that time. Here one of the early production Sea Fury Mk Xs, TF898, is engaged in deck-landing and catapult-launch evaluation on board HMS *Illustrious* for 778 NAS, March 1947.

Lt-Cdr J. G. Baldwin DSC	Fleet requirements duties.
Lt A. Haslam	Temporary fleet requirements unit established for Home Fleet's 1949 Spring Cruise in Mediterranean.
Lt- Cdr R. H P. Carver DSC, Lt-Cdr F. R. A. Turnbull DSC* (16/01/48)	Service Trials/Carrier Trials Unit.
Lt L. W. A. Barrington, Lt-Cdr D. L. Stirling (19/07/50), Lt-Cdr D. H. Richards (09/07/53), Lt-Cdr M. W. Rudorf DSC (28/04/54)	Communications unit. From 1951 also operated Instrument Examining and Bad-Weather Flying Training Flights.
Lt-Cdr T. E. Sargent, Lt-Cdr C. C. Thornton (26/10/49)	Northern Communications Squadron.
Cdr R. J. H. Stephens, Cdr E. A. Shaw (21/04/48), Lt-Cdr B. H. C. Nation (16/05/50), Lt-Cdr W. I. Campbell (24/09/51), Lt-Cdr S. G. Orr DSC AFC (04/03/53), Lt-Cdr R. E. Bourke (08/10/53), Lt-Cdr R. D. Taylor (01/01/54), Lt-Cdr R. A. Shilcock (24/07/54)	Naval Air Fighting Development Unit.
Lt T. J. Harris, Lt J. D. Nunn (28/10/48), Lt K. G. Talbot (06/06/49), Lt-Cdr G. R. Callingham (26/04/50), Lt-Cdr B. H. Harriss (01/05/51)	Refresher Flying Training Unit.
–	General duties.
–	General fleet support duties. Civilian-operated.

Right and below: The last establishment to employ the Sea Fury on active duties was the Fleet Requirements Unit, based at Hurn near Bournemouth. Though not a Fleet Air Arm squadron—it was administered by a private company, Airwork Ltd—it seconded mostly FAA officers to undertake its flying programme and its aircraft remained in Royal Navy ownership. An interesting feature of these Sea Furies is the presence of aerodynamic fairings on the main undercarriage doors, as seen here.

SEA FURY

This page: End of an era: stripped of their useful components, the remains of Sea Furies—the Royal Navy's last piston-engine fighter—rot in scrapyards at Church Crookham (top) and Lasham in Hampshire in the late 1960s; in the photograph at centre, the remnants of Hawker Hunters can also be seen. It was now the age of the jet, and the era of supersonic performance, sophisticated radar systems and air-to-air missiles.

SEA FURY COLOURS

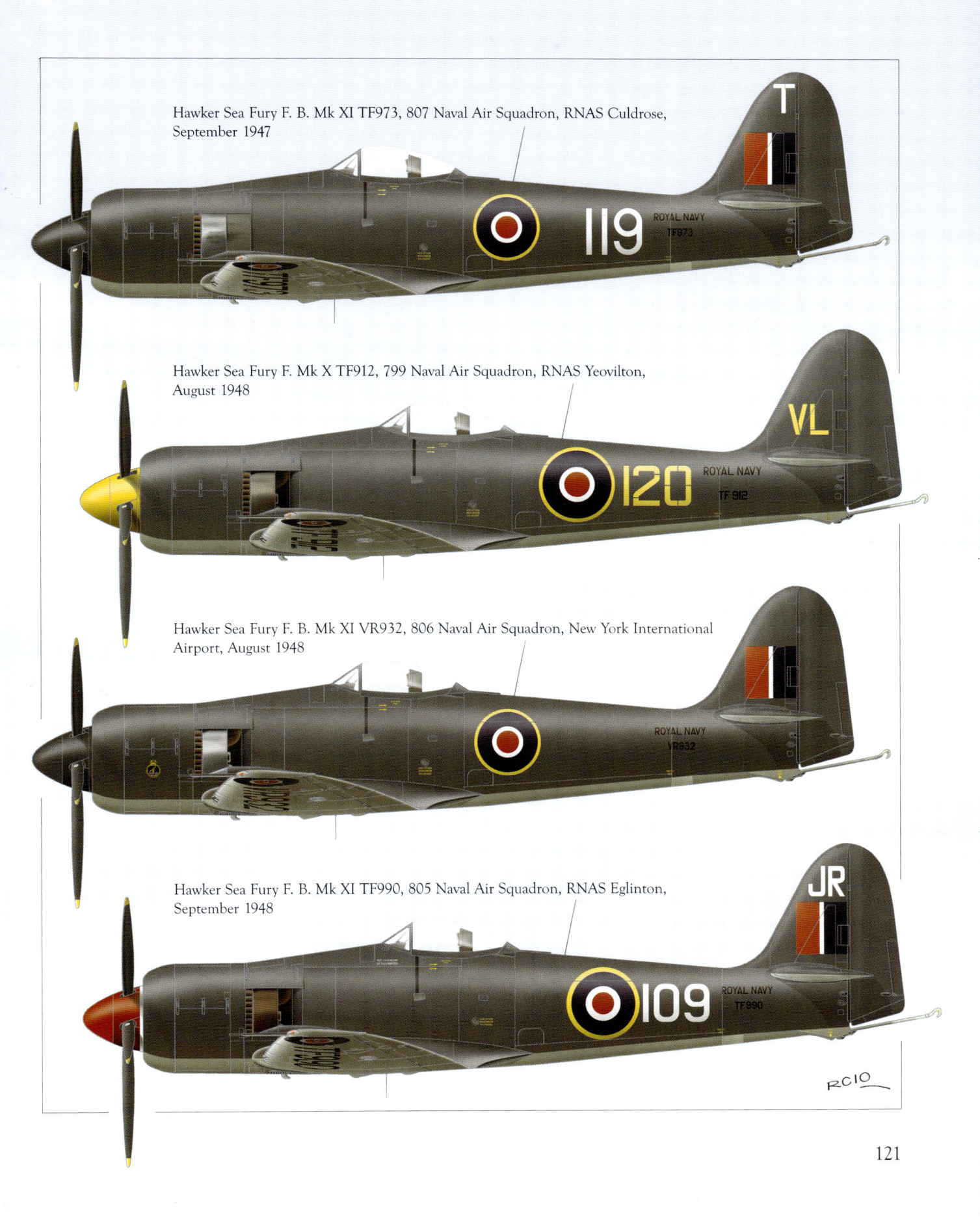

Hawker Sea Fury F. B. Mk XI TF973, 807 Naval Air Squadron, RNAS Culdrose, September 1947

Hawker Sea Fury F. Mk X TF912, 799 Naval Air Squadron, RNAS Yeovilton, August 1948

Hawker Sea Fury F. B. Mk XI VR932, 806 Naval Air Squadron, New York International Airport, August 1948

Hawker Sea Fury F. B. Mk XI TF990, 805 Naval Air Squadron, RNAS Eglinton, September 1948

121

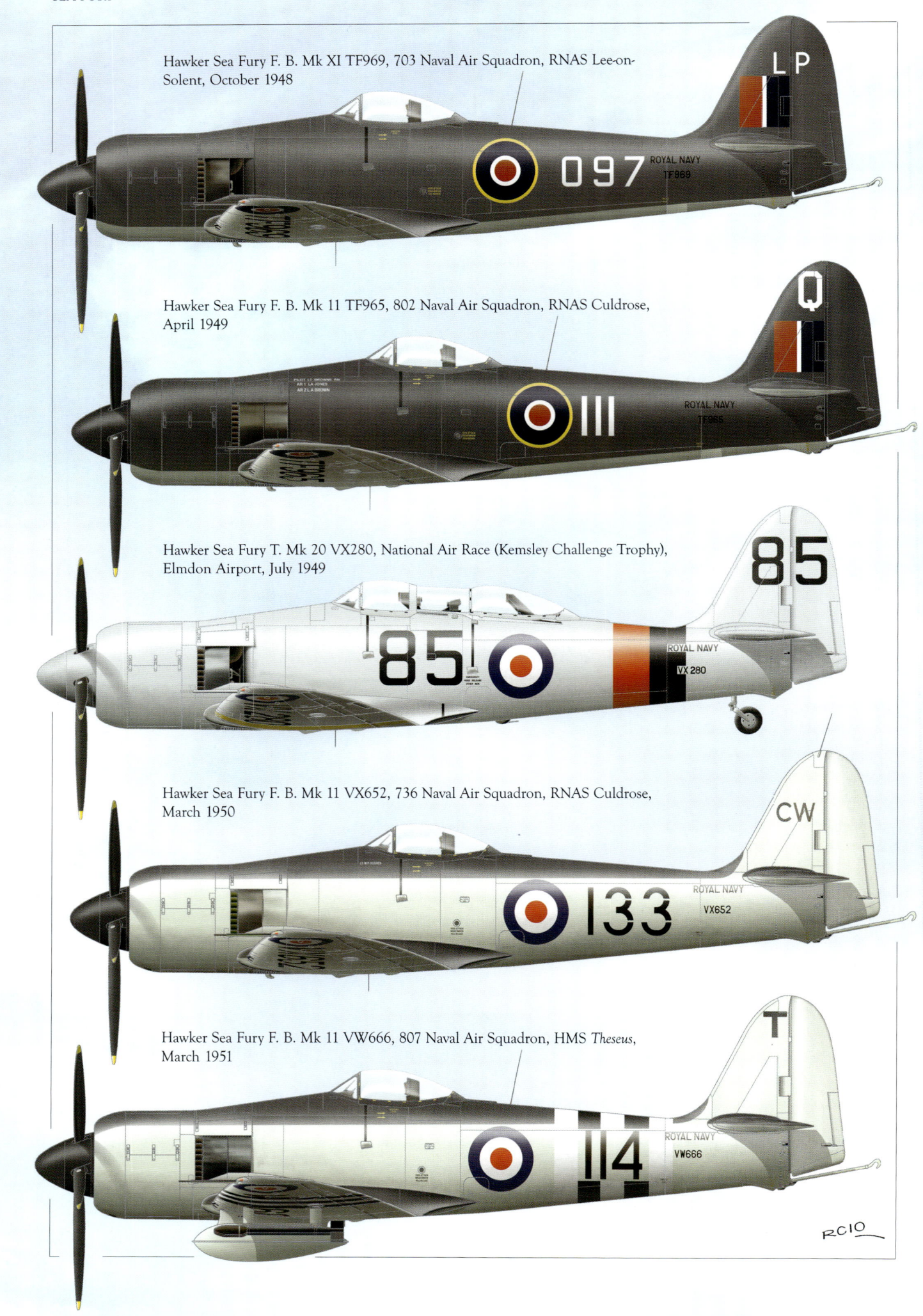

SEA FURY

Hawker Sea Fury F. B. Mk XI TF969, 703 Naval Air Squadron, RNAS Lee-on-Solent, October 1948

Hawker Sea Fury F. B. Mk 11 TF965, 802 Naval Air Squadron, RNAS Culdrose, April 1949

Hawker Sea Fury T. Mk 20 VX280, National Air Race (Kemsley Challenge Trophy), Elmdon Airport, July 1949

Hawker Sea Fury F. B. Mk 11 VX652, 736 Naval Air Squadron, RNAS Culdrose, March 1950

Hawker Sea Fury F. B. Mk 11 VW666, 807 Naval Air Squadron, HMS *Theseus*, March 1951

SEA FURY COLOURS

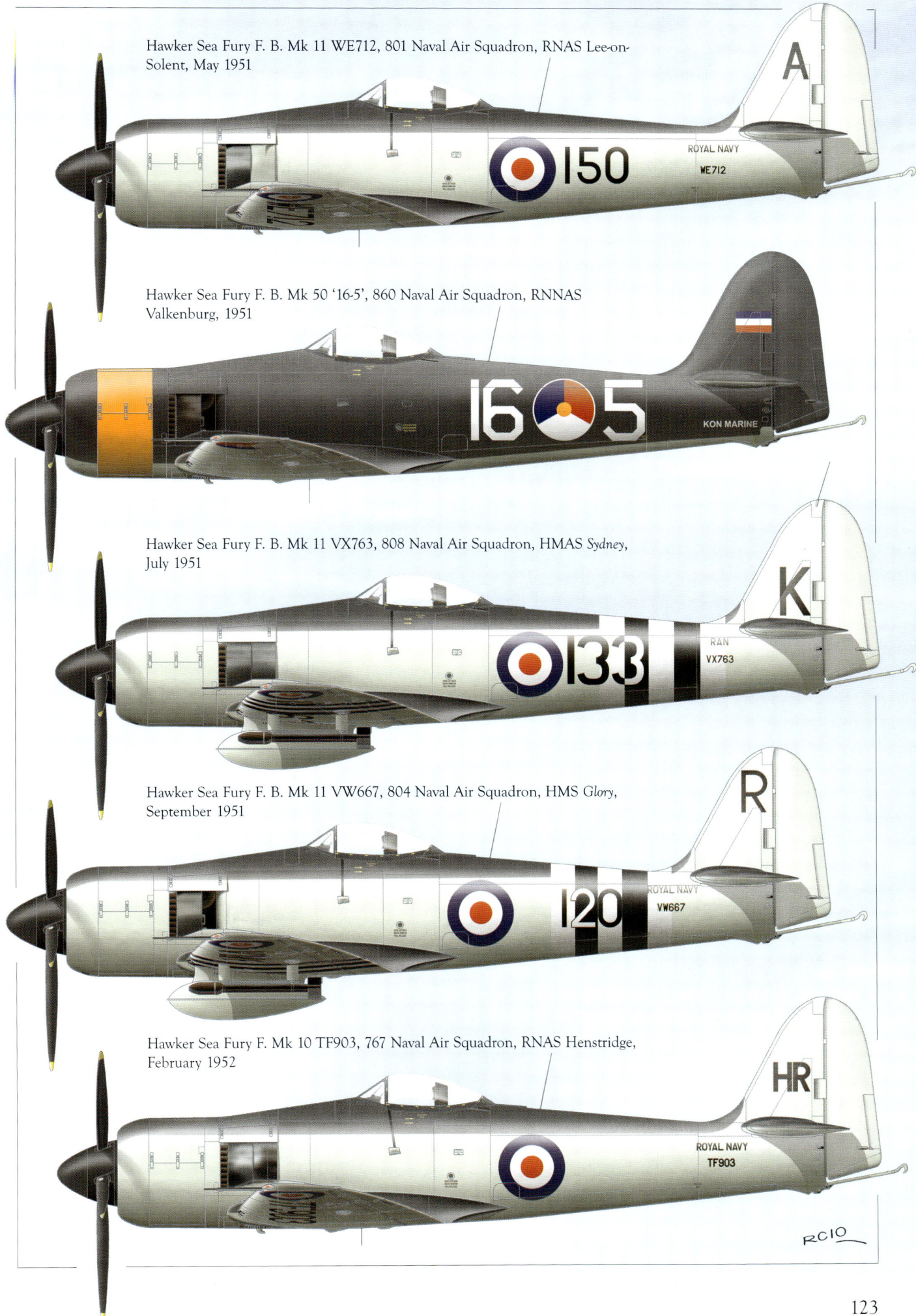

Hawker Sea Fury F. B. Mk 11 WE712, 801 Naval Air Squadron, RNAS Lee-on-Solent, May 1951

Hawker Sea Fury F. B. Mk 50 '16-5', 860 Naval Air Squadron, RNNAS Valkenburg, 1951

Hawker Sea Fury F. B. Mk 11 VX763, 808 Naval Air Squadron, HMAS *Sydney*, July 1951

Hawker Sea Fury F. B. Mk 11 VW667, 804 Naval Air Squadron, HMS *Glory*, September 1951

Hawker Sea Fury F. Mk 10 TF903, 767 Naval Air Squadron, RNAS Henstridge, February 1952

123

SEA FURY

FLOWN BY THE AUTHOR

HAWKER SEA FURY F. B. Mk 11
WJ295, 801 Naval Air Squadron, HMS *Glory*, December 1952

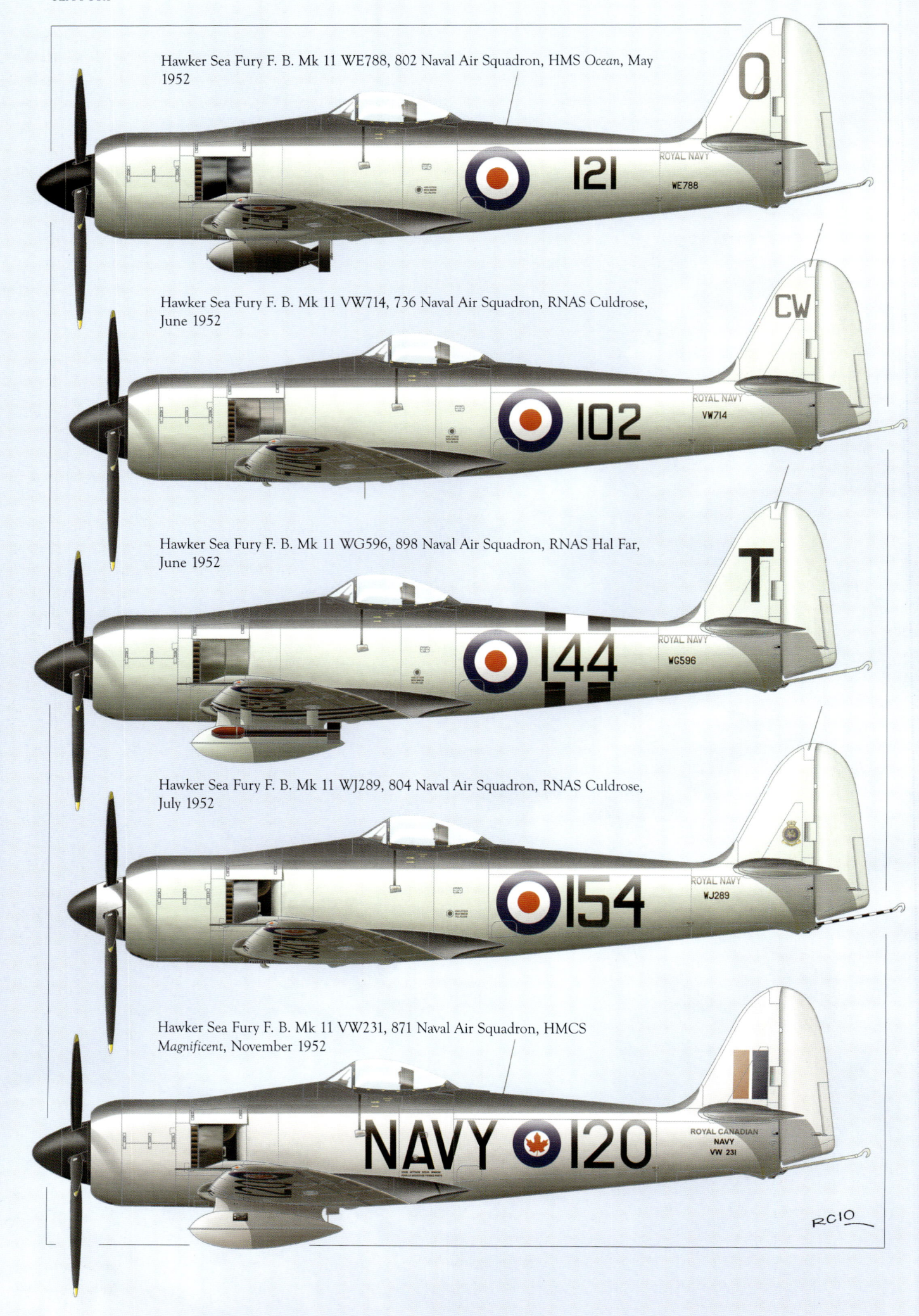

SEA FURY

Hawker Sea Fury F. B. Mk 11 WE788, 802 Naval Air Squadron, HMS *Ocean*, May 1952

Hawker Sea Fury F. B. Mk 11 VW714, 736 Naval Air Squadron, RNAS Culdrose, June 1952

Hawker Sea Fury F. B. Mk 11 WG596, 898 Naval Air Squadron, RNAS Hal Far, June 1952

Hawker Sea Fury F. B. Mk 11 WJ289, 804 Naval Air Squadron, RNAS Culdrose, July 1952

Hawker Sea Fury F. B. Mk 11 VW231, 871 Naval Air Squadron, HMCS *Magnificent*, November 1952

SEA FURY COLOURS

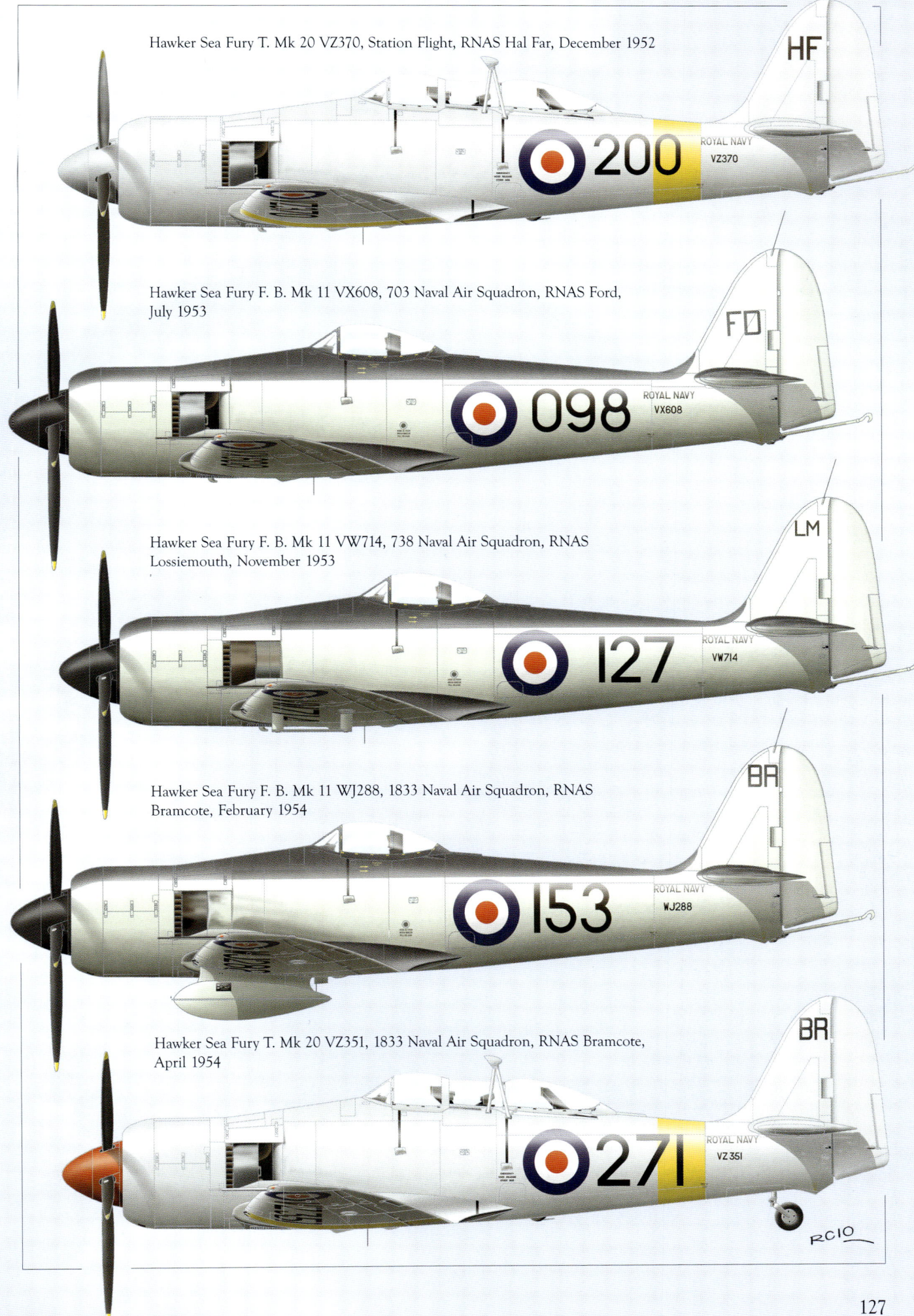

Hawker Sea Fury T. Mk 20 VZ370, Station Flight, RNAS Hal Far, December 1952

Hawker Sea Fury F. B. Mk 11 VX608, 703 Naval Air Squadron, RNAS Ford, July 1953

Hawker Sea Fury F. B. Mk 11 VW714, 738 Naval Air Squadron, RNAS Lossiemouth, November 1953

Hawker Sea Fury F. B. Mk 11 WJ288, 1833 Naval Air Squadron, RNAS Bramcote, February 1954

Hawker Sea Fury T. Mk 20 VZ351, 1833 Naval Air Squadron, RNAS Bramcote, April 1954

127

SEA FURY

Hawker Sea Fury F. B. Mk 11 WE725, 811 Naval Air Squadron, HMS *Warrior*, June 1954

Hawker Sea Fury F. B. Mk 11 WH594, 810 Naval Air Squadron, HMS *Centaur*, July 1954

Hawker Sea Fury F. B. Mk 11 VX664, 1834 Naval Air Squadron, RNAS Yeovilton, October 1954

Hawker Sea Fury F. B. Mk 11 VX642, Fleet Requirements Unit, Hurn Airport, January 1956

Hawker Sea Fury F. B. Mk 11 WH587, 805 Naval Air Squadron, NAS Nowra, January 1958